Cold Steel:
Regimental Wargame Scenarios for the Western Theater: 1862-1864

By Brad Butkovich

Cold Steel: Regimental Wargame Scenarios for the Western Theatre: 1862-1864.
Copyright © 2025 Historic Imagination LLC
All rights reserved.

"Knowing that I was almost out of ammunition, my only alternative was to resort to the bayonet. I moved forward with the expectation of using cold steel, but was satisfied to find that the enemy had promptly left when they saw us making towards them. They gave way entirely in front of us, and after advancing some one hundred and twenty-five yards, and not being supported, I did not feel authorized to proceed forward."
Colonel Joseph W. Frizell, commander 94th Ohio Infantry Regiment on the Battle of Perryville.

Stock #: HI021
ISBN 979-8-9904149-2-1

Cover: View from Open Knob at Perryville. Looking from Parson's Battery position towards Maney's attacking Confederate brigade.

All images of personalities were taken from the National Archives and Records Administration or the Library of Congress and are public domain due to age and expiration of copyright. All modern images of the battlefield were taken by the author.

All modern battlefield images are © 2025 Historic Imagination.

This book may not be reproduced in any format.

Historic Imagination LLC
4025 Leeambur Court
Lilburn, GA 30047
www.historicimagination.com

Table of Contents

Introduction 3

How to Use This Book 5

The Battle of Mill Springs 11

The Battle of Fort Donelson: Breakout 19

The Battle of Iuka 29

The Second Battle of Corinth 37

The Battle of Perryville 49

The Battle of Stones River: Opening 61

The Battle of Stones River: Sheridan Holds the Line 73

The Battle of Wauhatchie 83

The Battle of Fort Sanders 91

The Third Battle of Murfreesboro 101

The Battle of Griswoldville 109

Introduction

The American Civil War west of the Appalachia Mountains was wide ranging and vast. Many historians consider it the focal point of the war, and where the conflict was truly won. Innumerable battles were fought there, both large and small. It was hard fought, from the banks of the Mississippi River, to the piedmont of central Georgia.

This scenario book contains rules to play eleven battles in the Western Theater of operations during the American Civil War. It is somewhat of a catch-all for scenarios that don't fit as part of larger battles, or that have not already been published in previous Historic Imagination volumes. Some are quite large, while others are just a few brigades, or even one each, per side. The battles are designed to be played with rule sets where the regiment as the basic unit.

No specific set of rules is required to play the games in this book. Each scenario includes a detailed map for placing terrain and scenery on the game table. Unit starting locations are clearly marked, as well as where reinforcements may enter the board. Time is expressed in terms of 10 minute, 15 minute, and 20 minute increments; easily adaptable to most regimental level rules. The scenarios also provide a detailed Order of Battle showing each unit that fought in that battle, including figure ratios for 20, 30, 40, 50, and 100 historic men per figure/stand. The Order of Battle also includes a rating for each unit, as well as the weapons they carried into battle.

I wish to thank Dan Masters, author of *Hell by the Acre: A Narrative History of the Stones River Campaign, November 1862-January 1863*, for his with the order of battle and unit strengths for Stones River. Also, Tom Arliskas, author of *Cadet Gray and Butternut Brown: Notes on Confederate Uniforms*, for helping me with the Confederate small arms at Fort Donelson. And finally, I want to thank the Jasper County Public Library in Indiana for helping me find a map for the Third Battle of Winchester.

I hope you enjoy the book. Have fun at the game table!

How to Use This Book

This book divides each scenario into several sections, but before we get into the details, I'd like to discuss the most important rule, called the **Golden Rule**. Basically, the Golden Rule is that if you, the player, feel that a rule or design feature in any way interferes or hinders with the flow of the game, then feel free to change it. This is not a catch-all for sloppy scenario design. Far from it. The maps have been thoroughly researched and recreated from topographical and historical maps. The Order of Battle has been painstakingly to put together from what records are available. Rather, it is a recognition that not everyone will agree on a rules modification, the strength of a unit on the second day of the battle, or the consolidation of smaller units for ease of game play. If you need to change some rule because you think it will make your game better, then by all means the Golden Rule is for you!

Here is a summary of each section, and how to adapt the set of rules you play to the scenarios.

Background

This is a short background history to put the scenario in context.

Game Overview

This section provides basic information on the game. This includes a brief summary of the number of units and how long the game might take to play. It also includes the size of the game table. The scale for each map is approximately 33 yards per inch. While this might seem unusual, the size and frontage of regiments in most miniature games are too large. Since the majority of players will have their units based on this incorrect frontage, the maps are designed with this in mind, fitting the maps to the actual frontages of the miniatures themselves. Those players that have units based on the correct frontage will still be able to use the maps with little or no modification.

The scenarios are designed for use with 15mm miniatures in mind. For play with 6mm figures, half the ground scale and distances. For 25mm games, double them.

Game turns throughout the book are expressed in brackets. The first digit is the number of turns for 10 minute based games. The second is for 15 minute based games, and the third is for 20 minute based games. So, Turn [7/5/4] would be Turn 7 in a 10 minute based game, Turn 5 in a 15 minute based game, and Turn 4 in a 20 minute based game.

Terrain

The terrain section gives a detailed description of the terrain on the gaming table. It highlights unusual terrain features and any special rules regarding them. There are, however, some universal features that apply to all the maps throughout the book.

Most woods are fairly open with little underbrush. Unless specified in the scenario, woods on the game table should only be one terrain type worse than open for movement. For visibility, they should be the lightest woods possible.

Another important aspect of this scenario book to consider is the movement rates of the units. Units moved a lot faster than most people realized, even through the woods. Most Civil War miniature game rules sets simply move too slowly to replicate, or even have the potential to replicate, the historical outcome. It is therefore highly encouraged to modify the movement rates of the units. While all sets of rules differ, it may not be too difficult to make adjustments. One simple suggestion is to add two inches to all the movement rates. It is simple and easy for everyone to understand. Another suggestion is for those rules that have a split movement rate. There is normal movement, and a chance for additional movement with a die role to see if the unit loses its formation. Consider allowing units to move the entire full movement rate with no penalty. Weapon ranges should not be modified. Again, this increase is just a suggestion, and can be ignored if desired.

The hills in this scenario book vary in size. The standard is 1 inch of elevation per level. However, some scenarios are fought where the terrain was gentler, and the elevations may be only 1/2 inch per level. This will be specified for the scenario. Model hills with gentle slopes where possible, gradually going upward from the base to the summit and not chiseled terraces that block line of sight.

Also, don't be intimidated by the complexity of the hill elevations in this scenario book. Most people won't be able to customize their terrain to exactly fit the maps. So, if the map calls for a long ridge, and you only have a series of smaller hills, then string them together to make the ridge. Always remember, this is a simulation, not an exact re-creation. And the whole point is to have fun.

Most of the fences on the map are post and rail, or worm fences. Most are easy to climb and take down. Most rules sets provide a penalty for crossing them, usually an inch of movement. There are also clapboard or paling fences on some scenario maps. Lacking horizontal footings for climbing, they provide more of an obstacle to movement and are destroyed upon crossing. In addition, the thin fence boards provide scant protection from musket or canister balls. They do not convey any cover bonuses to a unit stationed behind them. An example is pictured below.

Deployment

This section details the position and deployment of the units that are on the board at the beginning of the game. It also provides the time and place where additional units and reinforcements march onto the board. It then explains any special rules or historical restrictions for the units.

Unless specified in the scenario, brigade command figures should begin the game within an inch of a unit in the brigade. Division command figures begin the game within six inches of any unit it his division. The location of officers above corps command, if any, are written in each scenario.

Victory Conditions

This section highlights how to determine the winner of the scenario. Most of the scenarios involve inflicting more casualties upon your opponent than you take yourself. A few games assign terrain objectives that either needs to be defended or taken by force.

Common to all the scenarios is inflicting casualties on your opponent. Each unit has a Victory Point value. When a player eliminates, captures, or forces an opposing unit off the board they receive the Victory Point value. Victory Point values are:

- 1 Point for each artillery section
- 2 Points for each infantry regiment
- 3 Points for each cavalry regiment
- 3 Points for each mounted infantry regiment
- 3 points for each brigade commander
- 5 points for each division commander
- 7 points for each corps commander
- 10 points for each army commander

So, for example, if a Union player were to rout a Confederate infantry regiment, and that regiment disperses or exits off the end of the game table, the Union player receives 2 Victory Points.

Order of Battle

The Order of Battle section presents the strength of the regiments and batteries used to fight the scenario. Each regiment and battery have several values assigned to it.

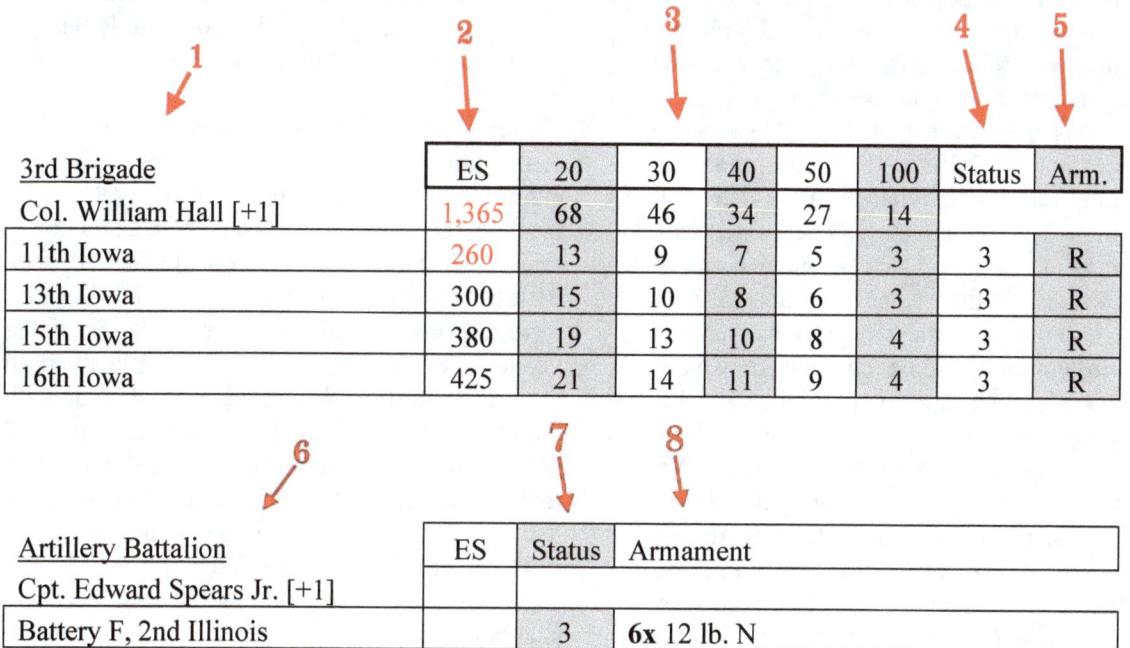

3rd Brigade	ES	20	30	40	50	100	Status	Arm.
Col. William Hall [+1]	1,365	68	46	34	27	14		
11th Iowa	260	13	9	7	5	3	3	R
13th Iowa	300	15	10	8	6	3	3	R
15th Iowa	380	19	13	10	8	4	3	R
16th Iowa	425	21	14	11	9	4	3	R

Artillery Battalion	ES	Status	Armament
Cpt. Edward Spears Jr. [+1]			
Battery F, 2nd Illinois		3	6x 12 lb. N

1. Lists officers, beginning with brigade commanders and upwards. The bonuses they provide to the regiments in their command appear in the bracket. Brigade commander normally have a +1, division commanders a +2, and corps and army commanders +3. Outstanding commanders may have a higher bonus and weaker ones a lower one.
2. Provides the historical strength of the unit at the start of the scenario. ES is Effective Strength. For Confederates, this is the number of men on the firing line. For the Union this would often include the officers as well. Numbers in **black** were taken directly from primary and secondary sources. Numbers in red are derived from simple addition or subtraction. Record keeping rapidly deteriorated during the course of the campaign, and researching the National Archives would not be cost effective. Also, because of the depleted strength of many regiments during the battles of May and June 1864, the scenarios combine many regiments into larger units for ease of play. Because of these factors, most regiment's strengths are, unfortunately, a best guess.
3. This section lists the number of miniature figures or stands needed to represent the unit on the game table. Again, this number can be either figures or stands. For example, if your set of rules has a ratio of 1 figure equals 20 soldiers, then you would use the "20" column. If your rules list a ratio of one stand of figures equals 100 soldiers, then you would use the "100" column. Also, feel free to adjust the numbers to fit the way you have your figures based. If your regiments are based in increments of 4 (8, 12, 16), and a regiment is listed as a "15", go ahead and use a 16 figure regiment to represent it.
4. This shows the status or morale of the unit. Values are given as 1, 2, 3, and 4. 1 is for militia and untrained troops and is the lowest value. 2 is for trained units that have seen little or no combat. A value of 3 is your average unit with a few battles and campaigns under their belts. A regiment or battery with a value of 4 has seen numerous battles and has generally prevailed in all of

them. If your set of rules only has three values, then combine some numbers, usually militia and untrained units. In that case, you will only need 2, 3, and 4. Giving each unit a value is a very objective task, though each unit in the battle was researched and an attempt was made to quantify how many engagements they had been in, and how victorious they were in them. As always, follow the Golden Rule. If you disagree with a value for a unit, change it. Also, for simplicity, feel free to assign one value to all the units in a brigade. This can make it easier to keep track of their values during a battle.

5. This column lists the weapons carried by each infantry unit. Some regiments may have used more than one type of firearm by company. In this case, the weapon used by the majority of the regiment is listed. We know what weapons were used by the Union regiments, but the Confederates left almost no record. Weapon types in red are a guess. If the quartermaster for the brigade or division listed smoothbore ammunition in their ordnance, then a few random regiments were assigned muskets.

6. The weapons types are as follows:
    a. R = Rifle-muskets
    b. M = Smoothbore muskets
    c. BR = Breechloading Rifle
    d. C = Muzzle loading Carbines
    e. BC = Breechloading Carbines
    f. RC = Repeating Carbine
    g. RR = Repeating Rifle
    h. Sh = Shotgun

7. Some rules allow for an additional officer figure to represent the commander of a battalion of artillery. If the rules played do not, then ignore this entry.

8. This column provides the value for an artillery battery, much the same as for an infantry regiment.

9. This lists the weapon types of an artillery battery. A detailed list of the exact breakdown of each type of weapon in the battery is provided. Players can then adapt that to their chosen rules. Weapon types listed are:
    a. N = 12 lb. Napoleon smoothbore
    b. P = Parrott Rifle
    c. 3" = 3 inch Ordnance Rifle
    d. H = Smoothbore Howitzer
    e. SB = Smoothbore gun
    f. JR = James Rifle[1]
    g. BR = Blakely Rifle
    h. Mtn. H = Mountain Howitzer
    i. 2.25" R = 2.25" Mountain Rifle
    j. WR = Waird Rifle

[1] There were three types of James Rifles prevalent at the time. Model 1841 6 lb. Guns rifled but maintaining their 3.67" barrel, Model 1841 6 lb. Guns re-bored to 3.80" and then rifled, and newly cast 3.80" rifles that resembled 3" Ordnance Rifles. Unfortunately, all of the 3.80" cannon were designated the same, regardless of the version. For simplicity's sake, I have labelled all three as "6 lb. JR". Would the 3.80" version with the Ordnance profile and longer barrel have had better ballistics? Probably. But without much tedious research to find out exactly which battery had which type, it's not going to make much of a difference on the gaming table.

One note about the units designated as sharpshooters for both sides. They were simply dedicated skirmish units, trained in light infantry tactics. They carried normal infantry rifles, and were not comparable to specifically trained units such as the famed 1st and 2nd US Sharpshooters in the east.

Optional Rules

Most scenarios contain historical restrictions and special rules to accurately play that portion of the battle. If you want to fight the battle in the most historically accurate fashion, and use luck and skill to try and change the outcome, then play the scenario as written. This section provides optional rules for replaying the scenario, more often removing restrictions to allow playing the game with more a free for all feel. For variety, one universal optional rule applies to all the scenarios. The players may disregard the historical placement of regiments within a brigade, and use whatever formation they wish. The location of the brigade itself should not change, but the formation of the regiments within can.

Map

All of the scenarios include two maps. One map shows the units with their starting positions at the beginning of the game, and numbers or letters indicating where new units enter the board. Each tick mark on the sides of the map indicates one foot on the gaming table. There is also a North arrow indicator. The other is a terrain map showing only terrain features. The default map for scenarios is 33 yards per inch map. Since the complete map can get quite cluttered with units on the board, the terrain maps will help with set-up.

A quick word about the maps. The main map is 33 yards per inch as a compromise between several game rules that can vary from 25, 40, to 50 yards per inch. 33 yards per inch also conveniently works out to roughly 1 inch per 100 feet of elevation, which makes map-making easier. Many of the maps cram a lot of action into a small space. While this is historically accurate, it can make for a cramped game. Also, because of the variation between the basing of units in many sets of rules, not all the units on the map may fit in the designated space. For example, one rules set may specify four 1" stands per regiment, while another may use five 1" stands for a unit of the same strength. Obviously, that would throw off the ability to fit every unit in the space allocated on the map. **Use the Golden Rule liberally!** If you are setting up the scenario, and you feel you need more room, adjust the map. Make a 3' x 4' map into a 4' x 5' or 4' x 6' map. Make it work! This is supposed to be fun! Below is a legend for the maps used in this book.

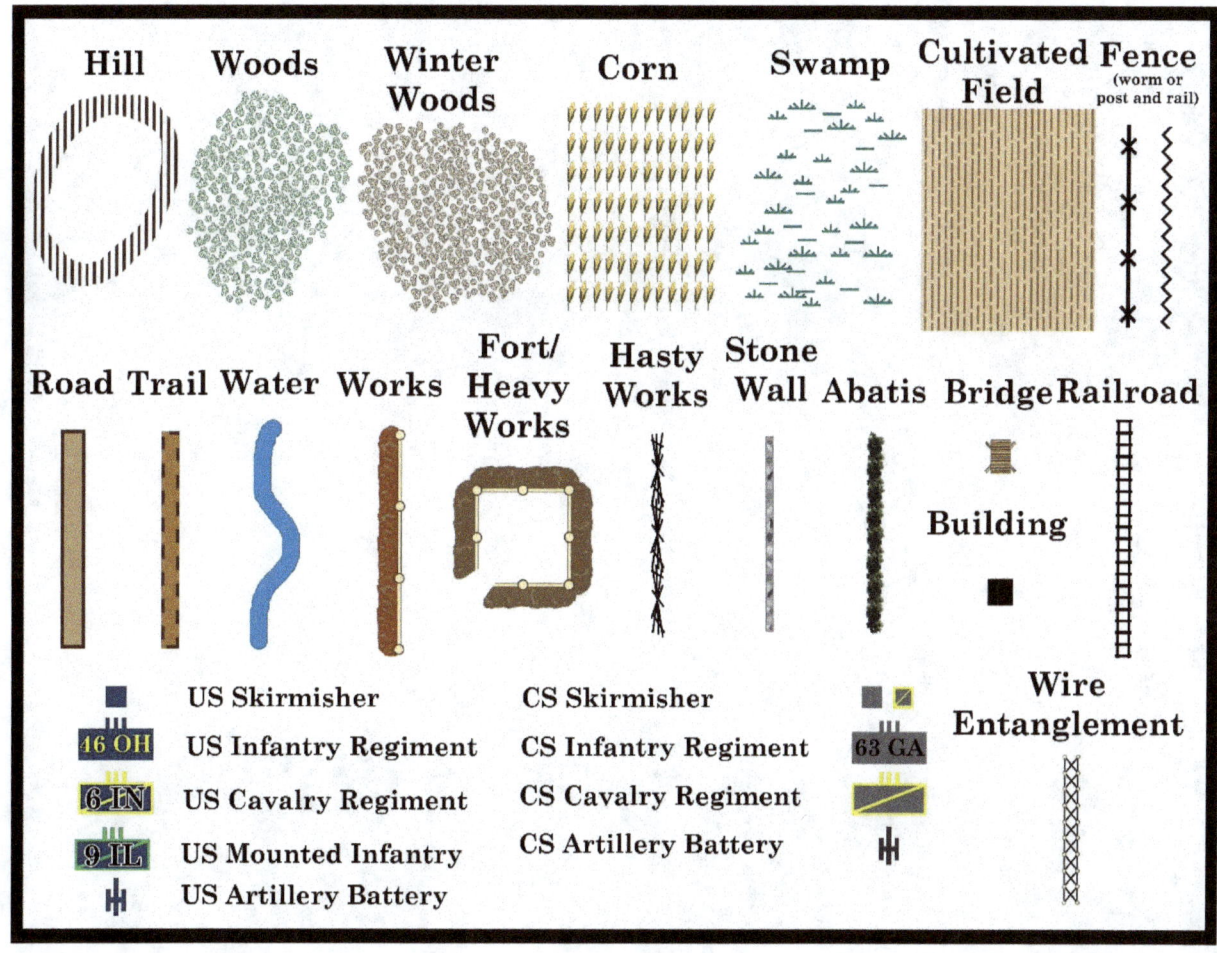

The Battle of Mill Springs
January 19th, 1862

Background

After the Confederates fired on Fort Sumter in April 1861, the state of Kentucky struggled to maintain a position of neutrality. While a slave state, many of its citizens nonetheless harbored deep Unionist sentiments. The state government declared the state neutral in the growing conflict. However, it was a fragile affair. Volunteers from both sides crossed state lines into Tennessee and north of the Ohio River, and enlisted in their respective armies. After the summer elections, Union recruitment camps emerged in the state itself.

The veil of neutrality was shattered when Confederate Major General Leonidas Polk crossed the Kentucky state line and occupied Columbus along the Mississippi River. From there both sides quickly occupied the state. General Albert S. Johnston, commanding the Confederate Western Department, established a line north of the Tennessee border from Cumberland Gap in the Appalachians, to Columbus along the Mississippi. The line was long, stretched thin, and only held strongly at specific points.

Confederate Brigadier General Felix K. Zollicoffer, guarding Cumberland Gap, advanced his command north to take a position near Somerset. He felt it was more defensible terrain, and closer to Johnston and his large garrison at Bowling Green. Both Johnston and Zollicoffer's immediate superior, Major General George B. Crittenden, ordered him to return south. However, at the time Zollicoffer was unable to comply because of the river and available transports.

Union Brigadier General George H. Thomas received orders to throw Zollicoffer back across the river. In mid-January he moved south through eastern Kentucky, and arrived at the small settlement of Logan's Crossroads on January 17th. Crittenden himself moved north as well, joining Zollicoffer and determining to strike Thomas before Union reinforcements arrived.

Brigadier General George H. Thomas

The rebels marched north on the 18th, with Crittenden planning to attack Thomas the next morning. Zollicoffer's brigade led the way, followed by a second brigade commanded by Brigadier General William H. Carroll.

It was a wet, miserable rainy night. The progress of the march for the untried soldiers was slow, and the Confederates stumbled upon Union outposts at dawn three miles south of Logan's Crossroads. The Confederates attacked, and drove them a mile further north. Meanwhile, breathless Federal messengers informed higher command of the enemy's approach. Colonel Mahlon D. Manson, the nearest brigade commander, sent troops south to meet the threat, but instead of sending a courier to inform Thomas, went himself. Upon hearing the report, Thomas rebuked Manson and ordered him to join his men. Everybody was learning their new craft that morning.

The first Federal unit to arrive was the 10th Indiana, which deployed alongside the beleaguered 1st Kentucky Cavalry (Union) delaying the Confederates. Zollicoffer continued his attack, and gradually drove the two regiments northward until the two Union regiments established a firmer position at the intersection of an old farm road. Here a slight knoll offered high ground, and a deep ravine to their left impeded Confederate progress. The fighting became heavy, but Zollicoffer's inexperience, coupled with the rain and fog limiting visibility, hampered the execution of a coordinated attack. In addition,

View along the Union lines looking northeast. The 4th Kentucky fought along this fence facing to the right. The Confederates marched out of the ravine, attacking from right to left. The old farm road was to the left of the fence from this angle.

most of the Confederates were armed with outdated flintlock smoothbore muskets. These lacked the range of the Indianan's rifles, and the flintlocks continually malfunctioned in the wet weather.

More Union reinforcements arrived, and the Union line stabilized. But Zollicoffer did not give up. The Confederates moved through the ravine and began to outflank the enemy line. Zollicoffer himself went forward to determine the Union position, masked by the rain, fog, and gun smoke. He stumbled upon a line of men, and thinking they were Confederates, ordered them to stop firing. The 4th Kentucky (Union)'s Colonel Speed S. Fry was nearing the crossroads of the Mill Springs Road and farm road, and encountered Zollicoffer. Neither realized the other was the enemy, but after a few minutes Fry came to believe Zollicoffer was attempting to trick him, especially after his horse was shot. Fry pulled his revolver and shot Zollicoffer dead, possibly with the help of a few infantrymen firing at the Confederate general.

Without leadership at this critical moment, rebel momentum stalled. Thomas arrived at about this time, and called forward the remainder of his division. Crittenden, farther to the rear with Carroll and his brigade, belatedly ordered his last unit forward. The combined mass of Carroll's brigade and Zollicoffer's remnants moved to again outflank the Union left, but the Federals arriving down the old farm road outflanked them and threw them back. Another assault on the Confederate right by the 9th Ohio broke their main line. The rebels briefly held on the next ridge to the south, but soon they were driven off. They did not stop until they reached the south side of the Cumberland River. Thomas followed, and when he crossed the river, the Confederates were gone. Crittenden's army had, almost literally, melted away.

The Confederate Kentucky line had been pierced. Events to the west would soon shatter it.

Game Overview

This is a small, early war battle, with essentially two brigades per side. It should be easily played in one session.

The map is 3' x 4' in size. The battle starts at 7:00 a.m. and ends when either side is forced from the board.

Looking down into the ravine from the Union line along the fence bordering the old farm road.

Brigadier General Felix K. Zollicoffer

Terrain

The map is small and hilly. The elevations should be ½ inches tall, but relatively steep. Deduct an inch of movement going up slopes. If needing to simplify, consider removing the lower level 1 elevation from the map.

The winter woods are open and light, and only deduct an inch from movement. The creeks are swollen from the current and recent rain, and deduct 2 inches from movement. The fences also cost an inch of movement to cross.

The real limiting factor for the game is the weather. It is raining during the battle. Deduct an additional penalty from any unit armed with flintlock muskets for the rain, on top of any penalty already in the rules. It is also foggy. Visibility is the same as heavy woods. Visibility will not improve for the duration of the game due to the fog, the rain, and the battle smoke that has nowhere to go.

Deployment

The game begins with the units set up on the board as shown on the scenario map. The 1st Kentucky Cavalry (Union) begins dismounted. The Union have no brigade commander on the board to begin with.

The rest of Manson's brigade arrives in march column on the Mill Springs Road at **1** on Turn [5/4/3] including Manson, the 4th Kentucky (Union) and Battery C, 1st Ohio. They will have to fight it out until Thomas arrives on Turn [14/10/8] on the Mill Springs Road at **1**. McCook's brigade and Battery B, 1st Ohio arrive on the Mill Springs Road at **1** on Turn [16/11/8]. Finally, Carter's brigade and the 9th Ohio Battery arrives at **2** on the Old Farm Road on Turn [19/13/10].

The Confederates converge earlier. The rest of Zollicoffer's brigade and Zollicoffer himself march on the board at **3** on Turn [1/1/1]. They are deployed in line of battle behind the front rank. Rutledge's Tennessee Battery follows them when there is room. General Crittenden and Carroll's brigade arrive on the board at **3** on Turn [13/9/7]. They can arrive either in march column on the road, or deployed in line of battle as the players see fit and the needs of the tactical situation.

Finally, the Confederate cavalry arrive to the left of **3** on Turn [20/14/11] to guard the flank.

Victory Conditions

The game continues until one side is forced from the board according to the command and control rules for the rules set being played. If the game ends before a definitive resolution, add up the Victory Points for enemy units lost. The side with the most Victory Points wins.

Order of Battle

Army of the Ohio

First Division
BG George H. Thomas [+2]

Second Brigade	ES	20	30	40	50	100	Status	Arm.
Col. Mahlon D. Manson [+1]	1,110	56	37	28	22	11		
10th Indiana	710	36	24	18	14	7	3	R
4th Kentucky	400	20	13	10	8	4	2	M

Third Brigade	ES	20	30	40	50	100	Status	Arm.
Col. Robert L. McCook [+1]	1,222	61	41	31	24	12		
2nd Minnesota	600	30	20	15	12	6	2	M
9th Ohio	622	31	21	16	12	6	3	M

Twelfth Brigade	ES	20	30	40	50	100	Status	Arm.
Col. Samuel P. Carter [+1]	1,780	89	59	45	36	18		
12th Kentucky	478	24	16	12	10	5	2	M
1st Tennessee	610	31	20	15	12	6	2	M
2nd Tennessee	442	22	15	11	9	4	2	M
1st Kentucky Cavalry	250	13	8	6	5	3	2	BR

Artillery	ES	Status	Armament
Battery B, 1st Ohio	122	2	**6x** 6 lb. JR
Battery C, 1st Ohio	110	2	**4x** 6 lb. JR, **2x** 6 lb. SB
9th Ohio Battery	104	2	**2x** 10 lb. P, **2x** 12 lb. H

Looking down the old farm road toward its intersection with the Mill Springs Road at the hilltop in the distance. Carter's brigade flanked the Confederate line here and drove the rebels back down into the ravine at left.

District of East Tennessee

MG George B. Crittenden [+2]

First Brigade	ES	20	30	40	50	100	Status	Arm.
BG Felix K. Zollicoffer [+1]	2,907	145	97	73	58	29		
15th Mississippi	854	43	28	21	17	9	2	R
19th Tennessee	676	34	23	17	14	7	2	M(f)
20th Tennessee	694	35	23	17	14	7	2	M(f)
25th Tennessee	683	34	23	17	14	7	2	M(f)

Artillery	ES	Status	Armament					
Rutledge's Tennessee Battery	140	2	**4x** 6 lb. SB, **2x** 12 lb. H					

Second Brigade	ES	20	30	40	50	100	Status	Arm.
BG William H. Carroll [+1]	2,560	128	85	64	51	26		
16th Alabama	330	17	11	8	7	3	2	M(f)
17th Tennessee	338	17	11	8	7	3	2	M(f)
28th Tennessee	748	37	25	19	15	7	2	M(f)
29th Tennessee	493	25	16	12	10	5	2	R
4th Tennessee Cavalry Bn.	336	17	11	8	7	3	2	Sh
5th Tennessee Cavalry Bn.	315	16	11	8	6	3	2	Sh

Optional Rules

This game is a great opportunity to use hidden markers. In this case, for the literal "fog of war." Also, consider imposing a rule that a unit cannot charge an enemy unless they could see them the previous turn, or were fired upon. In the latter case, they would be charging at the muzzle flashes of where they assume an enemy unit is located. This rule would prevent players from unrealistically charging at empty geographical locations.

Author's Notes

I love early war games with green, untried regiments, poor firearms, and in this case, fog! What's not to like! Plus, there is often familiar names that will rise to fame as the war progresses, such as George Thomas.

The photos for this book were taken in the rain and fog. Just like the real battle!

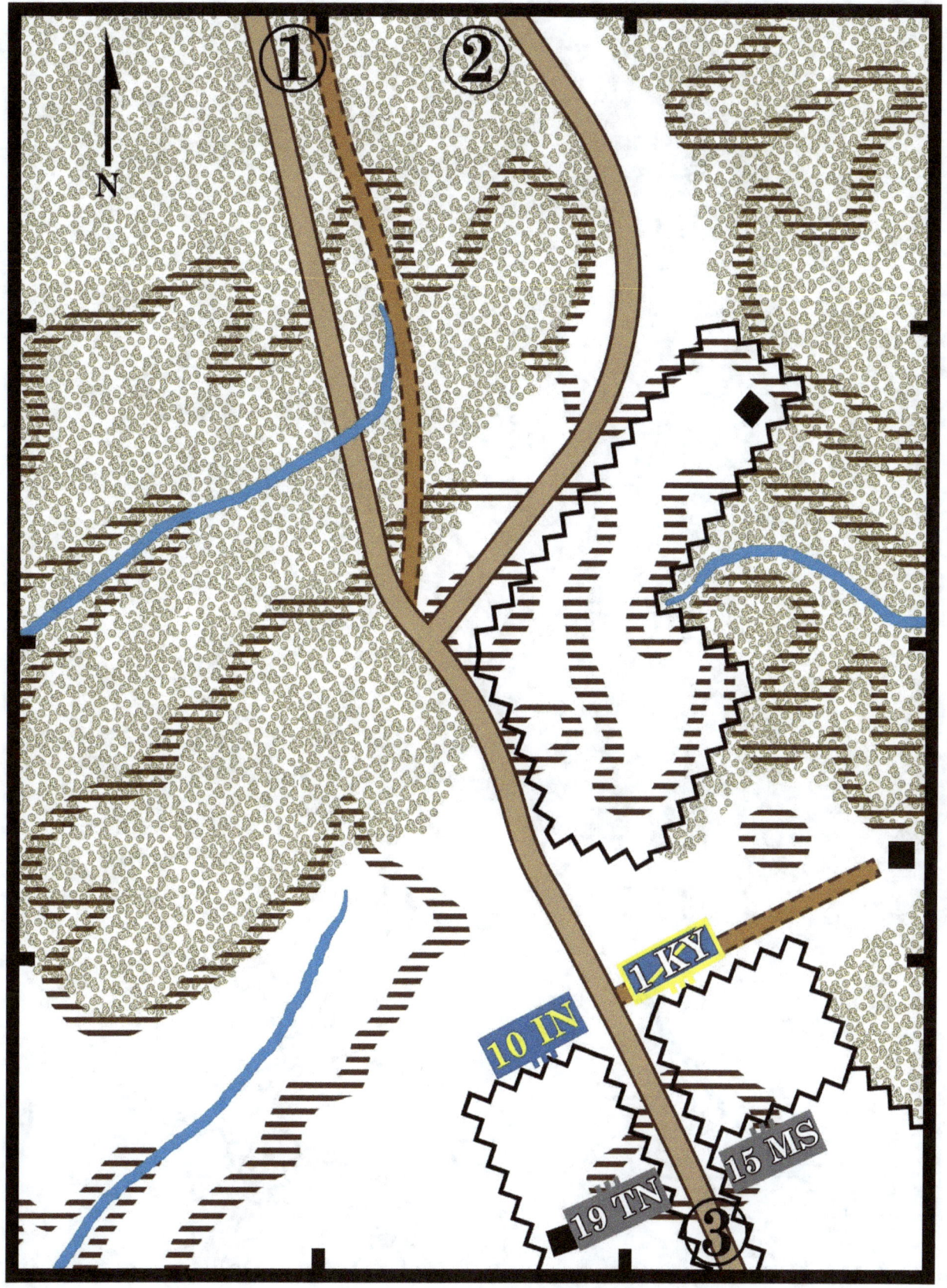

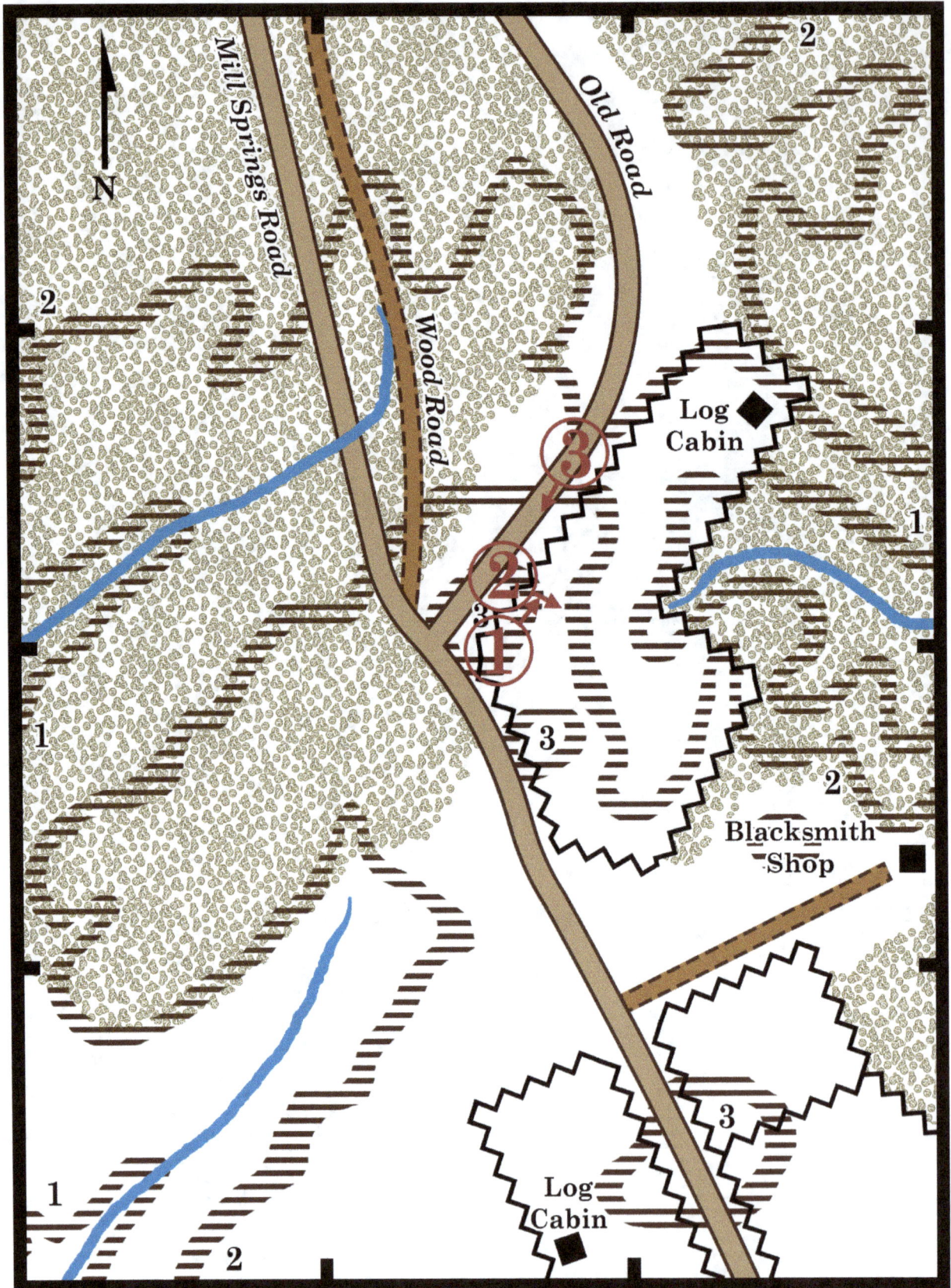

The Battle of Fort Donelson: Breakout
February 15th, 1862

Background

The defeat at Mill Springs pierced the Confederate's Kentucky line in the east, and Brigadier General Ulysses S. Grant determined to shatter it in the western part of the state. Grant had tested the Confederate defenses in November with a raid on Belmont, Missouri, but now had permission from his superiors to strike south. With close coordination and cooperation from the Navy, Grant first moved down the Tennessee River against Fort Henry. This paper tiger fell easily on February 6th. Grant then swiftly moved directly east to invest and capture Fort Donelson on the Cumberland River, eleven miles away. On February 12th Grant arrived and began investing the fort's outer earthworks.

The fall of Fort Henry spurred the Confederates into action. The Tennessee River was a dagger into the heart of the deep South, allowing river traffic access as far as Northern Alabama and southern Tennessee. Western Department commander General Albert S. Johnston ordered Columbus on the Mississippi River to be abandoned, and he withdrew the main army from Bowling Green to Nashville. Yet he wasn't willing to abandon Fort Donelson just yet, which would open river traffic on the Cumberland River to Nashville and beyond. He ordered 12,000 men to Donelson to bolster the garrison.

At the fort, Grant began investing the entrenched defenders. For much of February 13th and 14th Grant's men stretched their lines attempting to encircle the garrison completely, but without success. He had too few men, and had to call upon more reinforcements, which arrived shortly. The weather then turned for the worse. It snowed three inches the night of February 13th, and would snow again the next night. Union generals made several small attacks on the rebel lines without success, and on the 14th the Navy directly confronted the fort's river defenses. After a 90-minute battle, the Union navy was forced to retreat with heavy casualties.

Brigadier General John A. McClernand

Confederate leadership at Fort Donelson was complicated. Successive generals had been placed in charge of the garrison, and changed as new forces arrived and seniority of incoming officers prevailed. Brigadier General John B. Floyd eventually assumed overall command, with Brigadier General Gideon J. Pillow taking tactical control of the available land forces. During a council of war on the night of the 14th, the generals decided on an escape plan. It appeared the Union still did not completely surround the garrison, with the Union right flank nearest Lick Creek still empty except for skirmish lines. Lick Creek itself was swollen from the recent rains and snow, overflowing its banks and flooding the fords nearest the river. The Charlotte Road along the Cumberland River was cut off and impassable. The next passable road was the Forge Road upstream. The plan was to swing around the end of the Union line at dawn, gain control of the Forge Road, and march the garrison out of danger.

The attack started on time, but began to unravel immediately. As part of Grant's move to completely encircle the garrison Colonel John McArthur's brigade moved into position on a long hill overlooking Lick Creek the evening of the 14th. The surprised Confederates ran headlong into McArthur as they deployed out of town. McArthur fought back valiantly, delaying the Confederates. Next in line was Brigadier General John A. McClernand's division, whose division was soon hotly engaged with the

Looking east beyond Colonel Oglesby's flank. It was on this elongated rolling hilltop, Dudley Hill, that McArthur first engaged the Confederates and slowed them down.

oncoming rebels. McClernand sent for reinforcements from the division to his left, but Brigadier General Lew Wallace had no orders from Grant to help his fellow general, and delayed as he sought permission. But Grant was not available to send permission. He was downriver meeting with the Navy to coordinate the siege. Sending reinforcements to a fellow commander under attack would be second nature with more experience as the war progressed, but this battle was a first for everyone. Only a second messenger arriving in tears spurred Wallace to move his division to assist. That left only one division on the far right of the lines directly under Grant to invest and watch the remainder of the Confederates in their trenches.

A fierce battle erupted over control of the Forge Road. Flanked by the main Confederate thrust, the rebels in their trenches directly opposite McClernand soon left their work to attack the Federals in the flank. This two-pronged assault drove the Northerners back, and secured the Forge Road. Unfortunately, at the pinnacle of Southern success, indecision struck. Instead of marching out the Forge Road to freedom, Pillow ordered the men back into the garrison. He told Floyd his men needed to resupply and reorganize before leaving, an excuse the flies in the face of all common sense and the situation on the ground. Grant was quick to exploit the mistake. Finally arriving at the scene of the fighting, he coordinated a counterattack that fell on largely empty air, but firmly completed the encirclement and trapped the Confederates once and for all. The garrison would surrender the next day.

Game Overview

Fort Donelson is a large battle, essentially corps sized. There are about seven brigades per side. The Confederates are massed and have the advantage of position, but the Union will receive heavy reinforcements later in the game. Another unique aspect is the snow, if the players wish to replicate a white table. It's also a somewhat long game if played to its full conclusion.

The game table is 5' x 8'. The game begins at 6:30 a.m., and ends at 1:00 p.m.

Terrain

The map is a series of ridges rising above the network of creeks (called hollows in the area). The main ridge of high ground has the Winn's Ferry Road atop the crest. This is also the main Union line. The elevations are ½ inches tall. They deduct an inch from movement. So do the fences.

Water is a serious obstacle on the map. The recent rain has flooded the river and deepened the creeks in the area. The streams deduct two inches from movement. Lick Creek is impassable where it is dark blue and thickest, except the ford at the Forge Road, which is rough terrain.

Visibility in the desolate woods is quite open, with the white snow actually improving perceptibility. Units can see up to six inches in the woods with no penalty. After that it is automatically area fire or comparable. Rules for seeing inside woods from the outside remain the same. The exception is that Maney's battery in the redoubt with Heiman's Brigade can see over the woods in the low ground around Erin's Hollow and see the Union position on the Winn's Ferry Road. Likewise, the Federals can see the Confederate earthworks. If the Union move behind the hill, or forward into the hollow, they will lose visibility. That also means Maney can see and shoot any unit marching down the road in column.

The Confederate works are medium works for most of the line. The artillery redoubts are heavy works. There is a small, hasty work in front of Battery D, 1st Illinois, but otherwise the Union did not entrench.

Deployment

The battle begins with most of the two armies on the board as shown. Porter's Tennessee Battery should be just outside of one foot distance from the opposite Federal line. The 26th Mississippi should be on the slopes just outside of normal carbine range from the 4th Illinois Cavalry. McClernand starts the battle in the middle of his line with William W. H. Wallace. Pillow and Johnson are with their divisions stacked up on the Charlotte Road, and Buckner is with Brown's Brigade. General Floyd is with Buckner.

Brigadier General John B. Floyd

McClernand does not realize how serious the attack is until McArthur is fully engaged. His division may not move freely until Turn [7/5/4]. Lew Wallace's men begin arriving on Turn [16/11/8]. Cruft's brigade is the first to arrive, in march column along the Winn's Ferry Road at **1**. Thayer's combined brigades, followed by Battery A, 1st Illinois, enter along the same road in march column on Turn [23/16/12]. Finally, Grant himself arrives at **1** on Turn [31/21/16].

The Confederates remaining in the trenches are not mere spectators. Heiman's Brigade may not leave the works, but may shuffle positions. However, Brown's Brigade is released with full movement on Turn [19/13/10].

Victory Conditions

The game continues until 1:00 p.m. on Turn [40/27/20]. To win the game, the Confederates must hold the Forge Road open from the Winn's Ferry Road to the ford at Lick Creek. To be considered open, there must be no Union units touching the road, or within 200 yards. This may be 4-5 inches depending on the game scale. Officer figures do not count toward this possession or disruption. If the road is open at the end of the game, the Confederate players are considered smarter than their historical counterparts, and march off the board to freedom. Grant may or may not be relegated to a backwater command, and Sherman, commanding the Army of the Tennessee at Shiloh, is surprised and overwhelmed by a Confederate army 10,000 stronger than history recorded.

Order of Battle

Army of the Tennessee

BG Ulysses S. Grant [+2]

First Division

BG John A. McClernand [+2]

1st Brigade Col. Richard J. Oglesby [+1]	ES	20	30	40	50	100	Status	Arm.
	2,841	142	95	71	57	28		
8th Illinois	613	31	20	15	12	6	2	M
18th Illinois	531	27	18	13	11	5	2	R
29th Illinois	598	30	20	15	12	6	2	R
30th Illinois	512	26	17	13	10	5	3	R
31st Illinois	587	29	20	15	12	6	3	R

	ES	Status	Armament
Battery A, Illinois Light Artillery		2	**4x** 6 lb. JR
Battery E, 2nd Illinois		2	**2x** 6 lbs. **2x** 12 lb. H

2nd Brigade Col. William H. L. Wallace [+1]	ES	20	30	40	50	100	Status	Arm.
	2,798	140	93	70	56	28		
11th Illinois	500	25	17	13	10	5	2	R
20th Illinois	612	31	20	15	12	6	2	R
45th Illinois	623	31	21	16	12	6	2	R
48th Illinois	577	29	19	14	12	6	2	R
4th Illinois Cavalry	486	24	16	12	10	5	2	BC

	ES	Status	Armament
Battery H, 1st Missouri		2	**4x** 10 lb. P

3rd Brigade Col. Leonard F. Ross [+0]	ES	20	30	40	50	100	Status	Arm.
	1,377	69	46	34	28	14		
17th Illinois	750	38	25	19	15	8	3	R
49th Illinois	627	31	21	16	13	6	2	R(p)

	ES	Status	Armament
Battery B, 1st Illinois	120	3	**4x** 6 lb. SB, **2x** 12 lb. H
Battery D, 1st Illinois		2	**2x** 24 lb. H

Second Division

1st Brigade	ES	20	30	40	50	100	Status	Arm.
Col. John McArthur [+1]	1,748	87	58	44	35	17		
9th Illinois	612	31	20	15	12	6	2	R
12th Illinois	636	32	21	16	13	6	2	R
41st Illinois	500	25	17	13	10	5	2	M

5th Brigade	ES	20	30	40	50	100	Status	Arm.
Col. Morgan L. Smith [+1]	1,339	67	45	33	27	13		
8th Missouri	680	34	23	17	14	7	2	R
11th Indiana	659	33	22	16	13	7	2	R

Third Division

BG Lewis Wallace [+2]

1st Brigade	ES	20	30	40	50	100	Status	Arm.
Col. Charles Cruft [+1]	2,623	131	87	66	52	26		
31st Indiana	727	36	24	18	15	7	2	R
44th Indiana	652	33	22	16	13	7	2	R
17th Kentucky	681	34	23	17	14	7	2	R
25th Kentucky	563	28	19	14	11	6	2	M

2nd & 3rd Brigade	ES	20	30	40	50	100	Status	Arm.
Col. John M. Thayer [+1]	4,435	222	148	111	89	44		
46th Illinois	653	33	22	16	13	7	2	R
57th Illinois	569	28	19	14	11	6	2	M(p)
58th Illinois	716	36	24	18	14	7	2	R
1st Nebraska	559	28	19	14	11	6	2	M
58th Ohio	584	29	19	15	12	6	2	R
68th Ohio	733	37	24	18	15	7	2	R
76th Ohio	621	31	21	16	12	6	2	R

Artillery	ES	Status	Armament
Battery A, 1st Illinois		2	**4x** 6 lb. SB, **2x** 12 lb. H

A generic view of the Confederate lines around Fort Donelson.

Fort Donelson Garrison
BG John B. Floyd [+1]

Pillow's Division
BG Gideon J. Pillow [+1]

Heiman's Brigade Col. Adolphus Heiman [+1]	ES	20	30	40	50	100	Status	Arm.
	1,798	90	60	45	36	18		
10th Tennessee	337	17	11	8	7	3	2	M(f)
42nd Tennessee	498	25	17	12	10	5	2	M(f)
48th Tennessee	455	23	15	11	9	5	2	M(f)
53rd Tennessee, 27th Alabama	508	25	17	13	10	5	2	Sh

	ES	Status	Armament
Maney's Tennessee Battery			2x 6 lbs. 2x 12 lb. H

Drake's Brigade Col. Joseph Drake [+1]	ES	20	30	40	50	100	Status	Arm.
	1,368	68	46	34	27	14		
4th Mississippi	521	26	17	13	10	5	2	R
15th Arkansas	465	23	16	12	9	5	2	Sh
1st Tennessee Bn., 26th Alabama	382	19	13	10	8	4	2	M

McCausland's Brigade	ES	20	30	40	50	100	Status	Arm.
Col. John McCausland [+1]	1,003	50	33	25	20	10		
36th Virginia	521	26	17	13	10	5	3	M(f)
50th Virginia	482	24	16	12	10	5	3	M

Wharton's Brigade	ES	20	30	40	50	100	Status	Arm.
Col. Gabriel C. Wharton [+1]	1,011	51	34	25	20	10		
51st Virginia	479	24	16	12	10	5	3	R
56th Virginia	532	27	18	13	11	5	2	M(f)

Johnson's Division
BG Bushrod R. Johnson [+2]

Davidson's Brigade	ES	20	30	40	50	100	Status	Arm.
Col. John M. Simonton [+0]	1,549	77	52	39	31	15		
1st Mississippi	331	17	11	8	7	3	2	R
3rd Mississippi	546	27	18	14	11	5	2	M(f)
7th Texas	360	18	12	9	7	4	2	R
8th Kentucky	312	16	10	8	6	3	2	M

Baldwin's Brigade	ES	20	30	40	50	100	Status	Arm.
Col. William E. Baldwin [+1]	1,353	68	45	34	27	14		
20th Mississippi	500	25	17	13	10	5	2	R
26th Mississippi	443	22	15	11	9	4	2	M(f)
26th Tennessee	410	21	14	10	8	4	2	M

Buckner's Division
BG Simon B. Buckner [+2]

Brown's Brigade	ES	20	30	40	50	100	Status	Arm.
Col. John C. Brown [+1]	3,749	187	125	94	75	37		
3rd Tennessee	750	38	25	19	15	8	2	M(f)
18th Tennessee	625	31	21	16	13	6	2	M(f)
32nd Tennessee	534	27	18	13	11	5	2	M(f)
41st Tennessee	590	30	20	15	12	6	2	R
2nd Kentucky	600	30	20	15	12	6	2	M(f)
14th Mississippi	650	33	22	16	13	7	2	M(f)

	ES	Status	Armament					
Grave's Kentucky Battery		2	**2x** 6 lbs. **2x** 12 lb. H					
Porter's Tennessee Battery	48	2	**4x** 6 lb., **2x** 12 lb. H					

Unattached Cavalry Brigade	ES	20	30	40	50	100	Status	Arm.
Lt. Col. Nathan B. Forrest [+2]	578	29	19	14	12	6		
3rd Tennessee, 1st KY Cavalry	578	29	19	14	12	6	2	C

Unattached Artillery	ES	Status	Armament
French's Virginia Battery		2	2x 6 lbs. 2x 12 lb. H

Optional Rules

One optional rule is to release Heiman's Brigade at the same time as Brown's. Another would be to speed up the release of units and arrival of reinforcements for a faster game. This should be done on an equal basis, such as advance all times 3 Turns, for example. All players must decide and agree before the game starts.

Author's Notes

Another early war battle, and a large one. Decking this table out in white snow would certainly make for a cool looking battle (did you see that pun? Did you?). The rebels need to strike hard, gain the Forge Road, and hold it against a powerful Union counterattack. It may take a bit longer to play than many scenarios, so make sure you have the space and time.

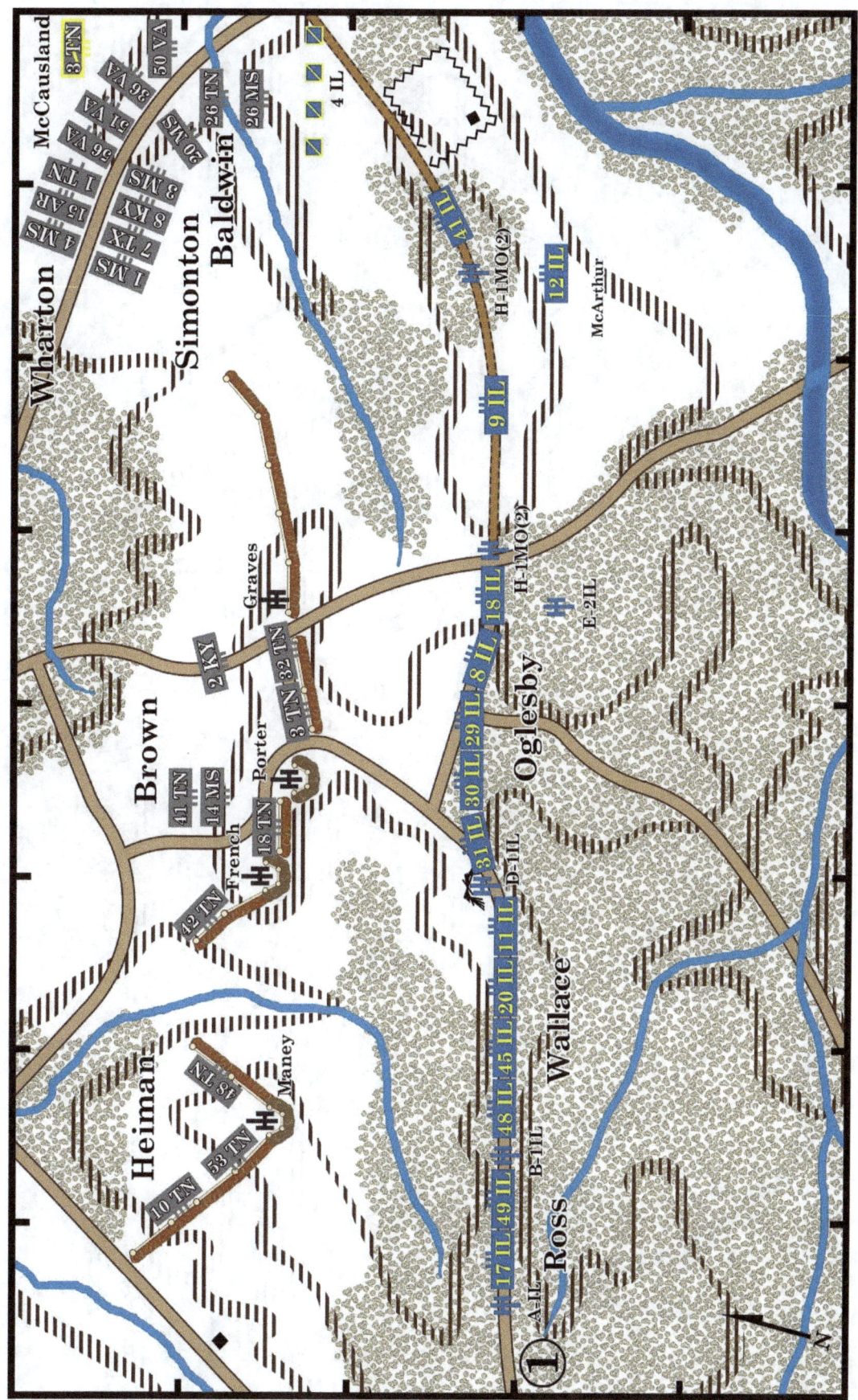

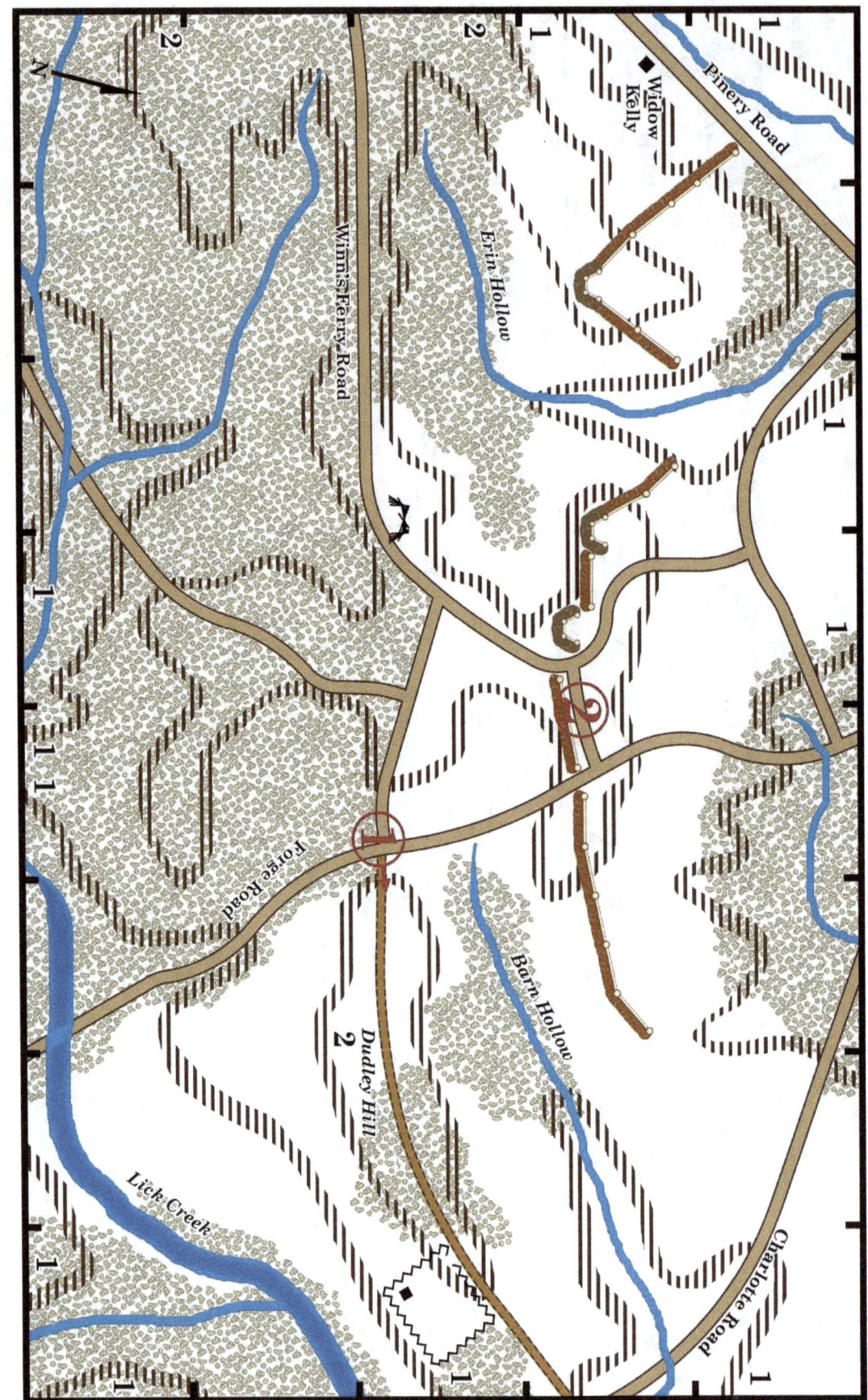

The Battle of Iuka
September 19th, 1862

Background

After the Confederates abandoned Corinth, Mississippi in May 1862 the large assemblage of Union armies broke up and went separate ways. Major General Don Carlos Buell's Army of the Ohio moved north to Nashville and then Kentucky in response to Confederate advances in that state. This left Major General Ulysses S. Grant's Army of the Tennessee and Major General William S. Rosecrans' Army of the Mississippi in the operational theater. Both armies guarded railroads and town in Northern Mississippi. The eventual aim was to m move south to capture Vicksburg and free the Mississippi River from Confederates control.

The Confederates needed to prevent either army from reinforcing Buell against Bragg's major offensive in Kentucky. Major General Sterling Price moved his Army of the West to capture Iuka in the northeastern corner of the state. It was the farthest outpost on the Memphis and Charleston Railroad, and a supply depot. The outnumbered garrison fled, allowing the rebels to capture numerous supplies. There Price awaited the arrival of Major General Earl Van Dorn's Army of West Tennessee. Once united, the two forces would attack Grant's supply lines in West Tennessee, keep the Union forces occupied, and prevent them from sending troops to help Buell.

The Federals knew Van Dorn was on the way to combine with Price, and moved to attack first. Both Grant and Rosecrans took the field and converged on Iuka, following a plan conceived by the latter. Grant would follow the railroad and arrive from the northwest, and Rosecrans would arrive from the southwest. Van Dorn suggested that Price abandon Iuka and rendezvous at Rienzi instead, seventeen miles to the east. Price agreed, and prepared his army to march on September 20th.

Grant marched on September 18th, and arrived about six miles from Iuka near nightfall. Rosecrans was delayed by a longer route and muddy roads. He promised Grant he could make

Brigadier General Charles S. Hamilton

up the time on the 19th. Rosecrans' forces arrived within two miles of Iuka by the afternoon. Noting Grant's timidity, who was in fact waiting for the sound of battle from Rosecrans to advance, Price shifted most of his army to meet Rosecrans. Brigadier General Henry Little's division comprised the bulk of the Confederates facing Rosecrans, and he struck first as the sun was setting. He hit Brigadier General Charles S. Hamilton's division hard. Both sides' deployments were hasty and haphazard, causing confusion and poor command and control. General Little was killed shortly after the battle began, adding to the Confederate command chaos. The Confederates enjoyed some success in the center, however, overrunning the 11th Ohio Battery and pushing the Union off the ridge. The fighting continued through the darkness for several hours, inducing a number of friendly fire incidents, until both sides stopped to regroup.

Due to an unfortunate acoustic shadow, Grant never heard the fighting to the south, and therefore did not attack the threadbare blocking force between him and Iuka. Price didn't wait for the two Union armies to combine and attack the next day. He left for Rienzi as planned in the middle of the night. The two Union generals awoke to find Iuka deserted the next day. Rosecrans pursued, but the Confederates had too much of a head start, and the Union too exhausted. The Confederate forces combined,

Looking east along the road from the Meeting House to the top of the ridge where the Union army was deployed. Unfortunately, most of the modern Iuka battlefield is either developed, or a major 4 lane divided highway.

and would continue to be a threat to the Union effort in northern Mississippi.

Game Overview

Iuka is a relatively small game, with a small map area. It can easily be enjoyed in a single setting. It also showcases low light and night fighting, as well as difficulties with command and control.

The game map is 3' x 4'. The game begins at 5:00 in the afternoon, and ends at 9:00 on Turn [25/17/13].

Terrain

The map is relatively simple, and mostly flat. There are two hills opposite each other astride the Jacinto Road on which the two sides are deployed. The road network is somewhat complex, but large fields also dominate the map.

The elevations are gentle, and are only ½ inches in height. If you can manage it, ¼ inches per elevation would work as well. The woods are fairly open and only deduct an inch from movement. Visibility is for light woods. Fences only cost an inch to cross. The streams are shallow and do not affect the game or movement. A unit may only get a cover bonus in them if it lies prone. The cotton field is just a nice visual effect, since we know historically it was indeed a cotton field, and does not affect game play. Overall, it's an easy board to set up.

The sun is low as the game starts. Twilight begins on Turn [7/5/5]. Complete darkness begins on Turn [13/9/7]. If the rules set played does not have night rules, consider the following.

<u>Twilight</u>
• Visibility in open changes to light woods
• Visibility in light woods changes to heavy
• Halve unit firing strengths

<u>Night</u>
• Visibility is the same as heavy woods.
• Quarter unit firing strengths.
• Halve movement rates.
• Impose a small penalty for attempting to reform from disorder.

Deployment

Set up the map and units where indicated on the scenario map. For the Union, Sanborn's brigade is together, but Rosecrans sent Sullivan's

Brigadier General Henry Little

brigade to the four winds. Sanborn and Rosecrans are in front of the 16th Iowa, where Rosecrans is about to upbraid his subordinate for some minor infraction with the deployment of the 11th Ohio Battery, and Sullivan is at the Meeting House. Mower's brigade enters at **1** in march column on Turn [10/7/5]. He can enter on either the Jacinto Road, or the farm lane next to it.

The Confederates are similarly deployed. Hébert's brigade is intact astride the road, but Martin's is split. General Little intended to personally lead the right wing of Martin's brigade against the forces around the Yow cabin, with Martin taking the left wing, but Little was killed early in the battle before he could take control. Hébert and Little begin the game along the Jacinto Road behind the 1st Texas Legion, and Martin is with the 36th Mississippi and 37th Alabama. The 3rd Texas Cavalry is in skirmish formation, and they are also prone. General Price arrives at 2 on Turn [2/2/2]. Gates' brigade arrives on Turn [13/9/7] at **2** on the Jacinto Road in march column.

Victory Conditions

The game continues until 9:00 p.m. on Turn [25/17/13]. If neither side has been forced off the board, add together the Victory Points for enemy units eliminated from the game. The side with the most points wins.

Order of Battle

Army of the Mississippi
MG William S. Rosecrans [+2]

Second Division
BG David S. Stanley [+2]

2nd Brigade	ES	20	30	40	50	100	Status	Arm.
Col. Joseph A. Mower [+2]	1,730	87	58	43	35	17		
26th Illinois	446	22	15	11	9	4	3	R
47th Illinois	497	25	17	12	10	5	3	R
11th Missouri	381	19	13	10	8	4	3	R
8th Wisconsin	406	20	14	10	8	4	3	M
	ES	Status	Armament					
2nd Iowa Battery		2	**4x** 6 lb. SB, **2x** 12 lb. H					

Third Division
BG Charles S. Hamilton [+2]

1st Brigade	ES	20	30	40	50	100	Status	Arm.
Col. John B. Sanborn [+1]	2,064	103	69	52	41	21		
48th Indiana	434	22	14	11	9	4	2	R
5th Iowa	378	19	13	9	8	4	3	R
16th Iowa	350	18	12	9	7	4	3	R
4th Minnesota	467	23	16	12	9	5	2	M
26th Missouri	435	22	15	11	9	4	2	R

	ES	Status	Armament
11th Ohio Battery		3	**2x** 6 lb. SB, **2x** 6 lb. JR, **2x** 12 lb. H

2nd Brigade	ES	20	30	40	50	100	Status	Arm.
BG Jeremiah C. Sullivan [+1]	2,147	107	72	54	43	21		
10th Iowa	462	23	15	12	9	5	2	M
17th Iowa	511	26	17	13	10	5	3	R
10th Missouri	650	33	22	16	13	7	2	R
80th Ohio	524	26	17	13	10	5	2	R

	ES	Status	Armament
12th Wisconsin Battery		2	**4x** 10 lb. P

Army of the West
MG Sterling Price [+2]

First Division
BG Henry Little [+2]

First Brigade	ES	20	30	40	50	100	Status	Arm.
Col. Elijah Gates [+1]	1,558	78	52	39	31	16		
16th Arkansas	421	21	14	11	8	4	3	M
2nd Missouri	358	18	12	9	7	4	3	M
3rd Missouri	366	18	12	9	7	4	3	M
1st Missouri Cavalry (Dismounted)	413	21	14	10	8	4	3	Sh

	ES	Status	Armament
Wade's Missouri Battery		3	**2x** 6 lb. SB, **4x** 12 lb. H

Second Brigade	ES	20	30	40	50	100	Status	Arm.
BG Louis Hébert [+1]	1,651	83	55	41	33	17		
3rd Louisiana, 14th, 17th Arkansas	489	24	16	12	10	5	3	M
40th Mississippi	314	16	10	8	6	3	2	R
1st Texas Legion (Dismounted)*	460	23	15	12	9	5	3	C
3rd Texas Cavalry (Dismounted)	388	19	13	10	8	4	3	Sh

	ES	Status	Armament					
Dawson's Missouri Battery	52	3	**4x** 6 lb. SB					
Clark's Missouri Battery	71	3	**2x** 6 lb. SB, **2x** 12 lb. H					

*Also known as the 27th Texas Cavalry

Fourth Brigade	ES	20	30	40	50	100	Status	Arm.
Col. John D. Martin [+1]	1,405	70	47	35	28	14		
37th Alabama	453	23	15	11	9	5	2	M
36th Mississippi	326	16	11	8	7	3	3	M
37th Mississippi	322	16	11	8	6	3	2	M
38th Mississippi	304	15	10	8	6	3	2	M

Optional Rules

There are no optional rules for the game.

Author's Notes

Iuka is a good, small battle that can be thrown together quickly. It also taxes command and control, which most players overlook in their games. Its normally fun to gloss over such things in favor of getting the shooting started and knocking down minis, but occasionally a game where mixed up and separated brigades and units can help understand what these 19th Century generals had to contend with. During a playtest, the two sides spent six turns (!) reorganizing their forces before even firing a shot! It's also critical to adhere to the night penalties for movement, visibility, and firepower to get a good feel for the chaos at Iuka.

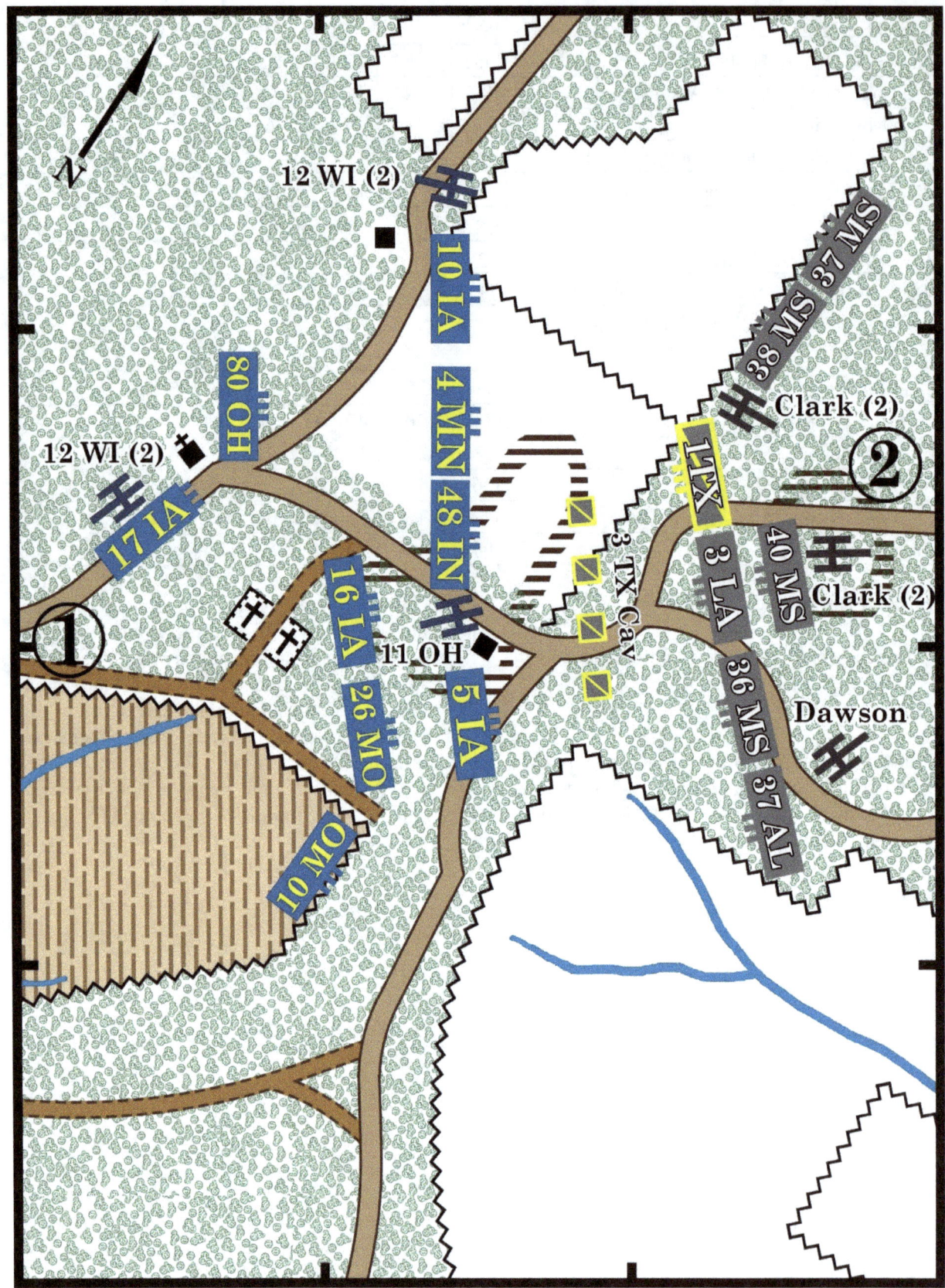

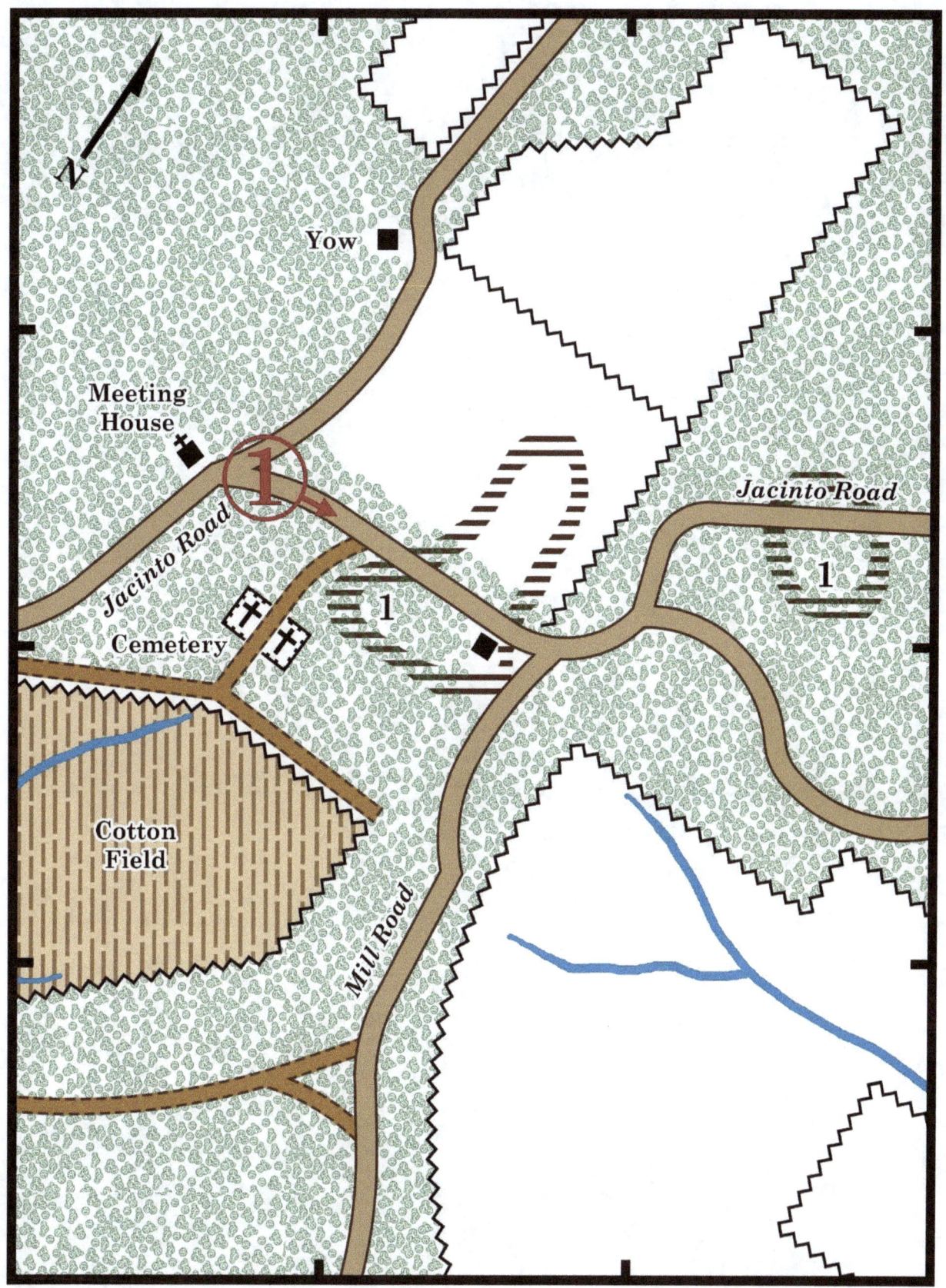

The Second Battle of Corinth
October 4th, 1862

Background

Following the Battle of Iuka, two Confederate forces united southwest of Corinth under the command of Major General Earl Van Dorn. The Confederates needed to support General Braxton Bragg's invasion of Kentucky, and prevent the Federals from sending reinforcements to work against them. Van Dorn therefore marched north from Ripley, Mississippi reaching Pocahontas, Tennessee, on the Memphis and Charleston Railroad on October 1st. From there Van Dorn moved east along the railroad towards Corinth. Corinth was a well-fortified town of strategic importance. It was a railroad crossroads, major supply base in northeast Mississippi, and had been the focus of operations in the theatre since the spring.

Major General William S. Rosecrans was determined to hold it for the Union. He wasn't quite sure that Corinth was Van Dorn's ultimate objective. Still, he began improving the inner ring of fortifications closest to the town. When the Confederates appeared before the town on October 3rd, the issue was decided.

The Confederates had heavily fortified Corinth during the spring, but their works were two miles from the town and concentrated to the east and north, the Federal's avenue of approach. Van Dorn was marching into town from the northwest. Rosecrans determined to meet Van Dorn at the old trenches, and the two sides fought viciously all day. Brigadier General Thomas A. Davies' division was particularly hard hit, sustaining the most casualties for the day and losing all three brigade commanders. The day ended with the Union manning the inner defense line. This line consisted of a series of strong fortified batteries, with an open area of felled trees before it to slow an approaching enemy. Rosecrans made efforts to connect the batteries with breastworks, but they were not completed before Van Dorn arrived.

The 4th began with the Confederates bombarding Battery Robinette before dawn, but the Union withheld their fire until daylight and

Major General William S. Rosecrans

better visibility. Once the Union opened fire, the larger and superior Union cannon quickly silenced and drove away the Confederate "king of battle," ending their contribution for the day. Van Dorn intended to attack as soon as it was light enough to see, but Brigadier General Louis Hébert did not attack, and his assault was the signal for the army to begin. Hébert belatedly arrived at Van Dorn's headquarters and announced he was too sick to command his division. His ranking brigadier, Brigadier General Martin E. Green, took over, but it was a further delay as he familiarized himself with his new role and got underway. The Confederate assault finally began just before 10 o'clock in the morning.

The screaming rebels smashed into the Federal line around Battery Powell, which was also the sector held by Davies' battered division. The shaky division folded, and the Confederates streamed up and over Battery Powell and the grounds around it, thanks in no small part to a faulty deployment leaving the right of the line "up in the air." Brigadier General Charles S. Hamilton's division lay behind Davies, and his men repulsed the Confederate assault, then turned and counterattacked towards Battery Powell. They successfully recaptured the fort, allowing Davies to re-occupy their former position. Another belated assault on Battery Powell made little headway.

Meanwhile a firestorm erupted to the west. Brigadier General Dabney H. Maury led his

Confederate dead in front of Battery Robinette after the battle. The cleared terrain in front of the battery is evident, with downed trees and brush present.

division directly against Battery Robinette. In a whirlwind of chaos, the Federals managed to hold the line, but one brigade broke through the left of Davies' division and entered the town. They got as far as the Tishomingo Hotel, but a sharp counterattack by reserves forced them back out. Rosecrans was seemingly everywhere, but his high-strung personality and exhaustion got the better of him. He ranted at retreating soldiers, and ordered supplies burned before the day was decided. In contrast, Brigadier General David S. Stanley held his division and Battery Robinette together by sheer force of will and courage, materially contributing to the Union victory.

At the extreme western end of the line, things were strangely quiet. Major General Mansfield Lovell was loath to attack the strong fortifications before him, so demurred and delayed while Maury's men were slaughtered to his left. Van Dorn called off his attack, and assigned him the rear guard for his retreating army. His hesitation did have the effect of holding his opposing division in place, negating both of their contributions to the fighting.

Corinth was held by the barest of threads, but it was a Union victory nonetheless. Northern Mississippi was secured for the North, and Van Dorn retreated to Holly Springs. The focus of the conflict in the state would shift in mid-October to the capture of Vicksburg along the Mississippi River.

Game Overview

This is a large, corps-sized battle that is evenly matched. It will take some time to play, so it is best for a convention setting or a permanent gaming area. The Union defenses are not so strong as to make this an assault on a fortified position, and Davies' battered division is a weak link in the Union armor. Overall, it is a well-balanced game.

The gaming table is 5' x 8'. The game begins at 10:00 a.m. and ends on Turn [37/25/19], if the game lasts that long. At 4:00 p.m. Union reinforcements arrive, securing the town if the Confederates have not already won and occupied it.

Major General Earl Van Dorn

Terrain

The terrain around Corinth is mostly flat, with gentle hills. Two ridges run north-south to the north of town. The slopes are very gentle, ¼ inch or ½ inch at most. It costs an inch of movement to go uphill. The woods are open, only deducting an inch from movement. The same for fences. The creeks are small and shallow. They do not affect movement, and only provide extra cover if a unit is lying prone within it.

The open are in front of the works is filled with felled trees. There was not enough time to construct a true abatis. The terrain is broken terrain for movement, or one worse than open terrain depending on the rules. Units in this terrain also get an additional cover bonus while traversing or inside the area. Any infantry unit moving through the area must make a tactical role or morale check, whichever is appropriate. If they fail, they go into disorder. This only applies if they are moving. Skirmish lines are exempt from this roll.

The town itself is an urban setting. Not every building is depicted on the map, although the western part of town has a higher density of buildings at the time. Do your best to fill it up with available buildings or declare the entire town rough terrain and blocking line of sight, except for the streets. The town is also conveniently enclosed by a fence.

The Union inner line is partially fortified. The batteries are medium works. The connecting works were not finished in time before Van Dorn arrived. The works in front of the 43rd Ohio and 47th Illinois are light works. The barricades in front of DuBois' brigade and battery are hasty works. If there is no difference between hasty and light works in the rules, then DuBois' men should only get an extra cover bonus. Two different officers later described their barricades as, "a few logs." The remnants of the spring Confederate line to the east of town are medium works, and appropriately, facing east. The railroads do not affect the game.

Deployment

The scenario map features the layout of the battlefield and the deployment of the Union and Confederate regiments. Half of Holmes' brigade has its flank "up in the air," while the remainder of Hamilton's division is formed at a 90-degree angle facing north. General Rosecrans begins the game at the edge of town behind the 7th Iowa. Generals Stanley and Fuller are behind the 63rd Ohio. Davies and Hamilton can begin anywhere with their divisions.

The remaining two regiments of Stanley's 2nd Brigade enter the board at **1** on Turn [29/20/15].

Corinth was a Union supply base at the time. There are supply wagons near the railroad and Tishomingo Hotel. The Union players can use them to resupply if any unit runs out of ammunition. Consult the rules being played, but most require the out of ammunition unit to come into contact with the supply wagon for a full turn to re-supply. The supply wagons can move as heavy artillery. Supply wagons can also be destroyed. A unit can spend an entire turn touching a wagon and it will be destroyed. Enemy artillery can also destroy the wagons as if they were limbered artillery. The supply wagons are always considered limbered. If the crew are "killed" by enemy fire, it does not destroy the wagon. It just remains stationary for the remainder of the game.

The Confederates are set up as shown. Some of the brigades have known formations and their regimental alignments. The others are up to the players. J. Moore and Phifer's brigades begin the game in attack column, or column of divisions. Price and Van Dorn begin the game near the Barton house.

The Confederate reserve artillery returns to the board at **3** on Turn [20/14/11]. Neither battery gets an initial or opening fire benefit, since they were engaged in the morning. General

Villepigue's brigade enters the map as reinforcements at **4** on Turn [25/17/13].

Victory Conditions

The game ends when the Confederates have compelled the Union to withdraw, the Confederates take so many casualties they cannot continue to advance, or Union reinforcements arrive at 4 o'clock on Turn [37/25/19], making a Union victory. If you really, really want to continue the game because it hasn't been decided by that time (and let's be honest, that would be one heck of a game), then see the Optional Rules section for their arrival.

Order of Battle

Army of the Mississippi
MG William S. Rosecrans [+1]

Second Division
BG David S. Stanley [+2]

1st Brigade Col. John W. Fuller [+1]	ES	20	30	40	50	100	Status	Arm.
	1,452	73	48	36	29	15		
27th Ohio	445	22	15	11	9	4	3	R
39th Ohio	357	18	12	9	7	4	3	R
43rd Ohio	375	19	13	9	8	4	3	R
63rd Ohio	275	14	9	7	6	3	3	R

	ES	Status	Armament
3rd Michigan Battery		2	**3x** 10 lb. P, **1x** 12 lb. H
8th Wisconsin Battery		2	**4x** 10 lb. P
Battery F, 2nd United States		3	**2x** 10 lb. P, **2x** 6 lb. SB, **2x** 12 lb. H

2nd Brigade*	ES	20	30	40	50	100	Status	Arm.
	1,976	99	66	49	40	20		
26th Illinois	431	22	14	11	9	4	3	R
47th Illinois	480	24	16	12	10	5	3	R
5th Minnesota	356	18	12	9	7	4	3	R
11th Missouri	305	15	10	8	6	3	3	R
8th Wisconsin	404	20	13	10	8	4	3	M

	ES	Status	Armament
2nd Iowa Battery		2	**4x** 6 lb. SB, **2x** 12 lb. H

*Under the direct command of General Stanley. Col. Joseph Mower, the brigade commander, was captured on the skirmish line early in the morning. No regimental commander appears to have taken over brigade command.

Modern view of the slope and northern face of Battery Robinette. The battery was located on the second rise in the background. This was the Confederate approach.

Third Division

BG Charles S. Hamilton [+1]

1st Brigade BG Napoleon B. Buford [+1]	ES	20	30	40	50	100	Status	Arm.
	1,881	94	63	47	38	19		
48th Indiana	324	16	11	8	6	3	3	R
59th Indiana	636	32	21	16	13	6	3	R
4th Minnesota	422	21	14	11	8	4	3	M
26th Missouri, 5th Iowa	499	25	17	12	10	5	3	R

	ES	Status	Armament
Battery M, 1st Missouri		3	**4x** 10 lb. P
11th Ohio Battery		2	**2x** 6 lb. SB, **2x** 12 lb. H

2nd Brigade Col. Samuel A. Holmes [+0]	ES	20	30	40	50	100	Status	Arm.
	2,609	130	87	65	52	26		
56th Illinois	583	29	19	15	12	6	2	R
10th Iowa	445	22	15	11	9	4	3	M
17th Iowa	455	23	15	11	9	5	3	R
10th Missouri	627	31	21	16	13	6	3	R
80th Ohio	499	25	17	12	10	5	3	R

	ES	Status	Armament
6th Wisconsin Battery		2	**2x** 6 lb. SB, **2x** 6 lb. JR, **2x** 12 lb. H
12th Wisconsin Battery		3	**4x** 10 lb. P

Unattached	ES	20	30	40	50	100	Status	Arm.
	385	19	13	10	8	4		
64th and 66th Illinois*	385	19	13	10	8	4	4	SSR

*66th Illinois also known as the 14th Missouri or Western Sharpshooters

Second Division, Army of the Tennessee
BG Thomas A. Davies [+2]

1st Brigade	ES	20	30	40	50	100	Status	Arm.
Col. Thomas W. Sweeny [+0]	936	47	31	23	19	9		
52nd Illinois	303	15	10	8	6	3	3	R
2nd Iowa	304	15	10	8	6	3	3	R
7th Iowa, (8th, 12th, 14th Iowa, 58th Illinois*)	329	16	11	8	7	3	1	R

*Consolildated unit known as the Union Brigade.

2nd Brigade	ES	20	30	40	50	100	Status	Arm.
Col. August Mersy [+0]	1,007	50	34	25	20	10		
9th Illinois	244	12	8	6	5	2	3	M
12th Illinois, 81st Ohio	390	20	13	10	8	4	2	R
22nd Ohio	373	19	12	9	7	4	2	R

3rd Brigade	ES	20	30	40	50	100	Status	Arm.
Col. John W. DuBois [+0]	757	38	25	19	15	8		
7th Illinois	310	16	10	8	6	3	1	R
50th, 57th Illinois	447	22	15	11	9	4	2	R

Artillery	ES	Status	Armament
Major George H. Stone [+1]			
Battery D, 1st Missouri		3	**3x** 20 lb. P, **1x** 6 lb. SB, **1x** 12 lb. H*
Battery H, 1st Missouri		3	**1x** 10 lb. P, **1x** 24 lb. H
Battery I, 1st Missouri		3	**3x** 6 lb. SB, **1x** 12 lb. H
Battery K, 1st Missouri		3	**4x** 10 lb. P

*The 6 lb. and 12 lb. cannon were attached in the fort from Battery I, 1st Missouri for the battle.

Sixth Division, Army of the Tennessee

Artillery	ES	Status	Armament
Cpt. Andrew Hickenlooper [+1]			
10th Ohio Battery		2	**4x** 6 lb. JR

Forts	ES	Status	Armament
Battery Robinett		3	**3x** 20 lb. P
Battery Williams		3	**3x** 30 lb. P

Army of West Tennessee
MG Earl Van Dorn [+2]

Price's Corps, Army of the West
MG Sterling Price [+2]

First Division
BG Martin E. Green [+1]

First Brigade	ES	20	30	40	50	100	Status	Arm.
Col. Elijah Gates [+1]	1,901	95	63	48	38	19		
16th Arkansas	407	20	14	10	8	4	3	M
2nd Missouri	322	16	11	8	6	3	3	M
3rd Missouri	345	17	12	9	7	3	3	M
5th Missouri	433	22	14	11	9	4	2	R
1st Missouri Cavalry (Dismounted)	394	20	13	10	8	4	3	Sh

Second Brigade	ES	20	30	40	50	100	Status	Arm.
Col. W. Bruce Colbert [+0]	1,301	65	43	33	26	13		
3rd Louisiana, 14th, 17th Arkansas	340	17	11	9	7	3	3	M
40th Mississippi	234	12	8	6	5	2	3	R
1st Texas Legion (Dismounted)	435	22	15	11	9	4	3	C
3rd Texas Cavalry (Dismounted)	292	15	10	7	6	3	3	Sh

Third Brigade	ES	20	30	40	50	100	Status	Arm.
Col. William H. Moore [+0]	1,689	84	56	42	34	17		
43rd Mississippi	314	16	10	8	6	3	2	M
7th Mississippi Bn.	268	13	9	7	5	3	2	M
4th Missouri	397	20	13	10	8	4	2	M
6th Missouri	342	17	11	9	7	3	2	R
3rd Missouri Cavalry (Dismounted)	368	18	12	9	7	4	3	C

Looking from the ramparts of Battery Powell towards the open field the Confederate's had to charge across. Note the sparse trees and stumps.

Fourth Brigade Col. Robert McLain [+0]	ES	20	30	40	50	100	Status	Arm.
	1,405	70	47	35	28	14		
37th Alabama	453	23	15	11	9	5	3	M
36th Mississippi	326	16	11	8	7	3	3	M
37th Mississippi	322	16	11	8	6	3	3	M
38th Mississippi	304	15	10	8	6	3	3	M

Maury's Division

BG Dabney H. Maury [+2]

Moore's Brigade BG John C. Moore [+1]	ES	20	30	40	50	100	Status	Arm.
	1,982	99	66	50	40	20		
42nd Alabama	365	18	12	9	7	4	2	R
15th Arkansas	312	16	10	8	6	3	3	M
23rd Arkansas	366	18	12	9	7	4	2	M
35th Mississippi	512	26	17	13	10	5	2	R
2nd Texas	427	21	14	11	9	4	3	R

Cabell's Brigade	ES	20	30	40	50	100	Status	Arm.
BG William L. Cabell [+1]	1,367	68	46	34	27	14		
18th, 19th Arkansas	562	28	19	14	11	6	3	R
20th, 21st Arkansas	535	27	18	13	11	5	2	M
Jones' Arkansas Bn., Rapley's AR SS Bn.	270	14	9	7	5	3	2	R

Phifer's Brigade	ES	20	30	40	50	100	Status	Arm.
BG Charles W. Phifer [+1]	1,306	65	44	33	26	13		
3rd Arkansas Cavalry (Dismounted)	315	16	11	8	6	3	2	C
6th Texas Cavalry (Dismounted)	352	18	12	9	7	4	3	Sh
9th Texas Cavalry (Dismounted)	435	22	15	11	9	4	3	C
Stirman's Sharpshooter Bn.	204	10	7	5	4	2	2	R

Reserve Artillery	ES	Status	Armament
Lt. William E. Burnet [+1]			
Hoxton's Tennessee Battery		3	**3x** 6 lb. SB
Sengstak's Alabama Battery		3	**1x** 3" R, **1x** 24 lb. H, **2x** 6 lb. SB

District of the Mississippi
First Division

Second Brigade	ES	20	30	40	50	100	Status	Arm.
BG John B. Villepigue [+1]	1,662	83	55	42	33	17		
1st Confederate Bn., 2nd Louisiana Zouave Bn.	355	18	12	9	7	4	3	R
12th Louisiana	451	23	15	11	9	5	3	R
33rd Mississippi	482	24	16	12	10	5	3	M
39th Mississippi	374	19	12	9	7	4	3	R

Optional Rules

If the game has still not been decided one way or the other by 4:00 p.m. with the arrival of General McPherson, the game can continue. McPherson's division enters at **2** on Turn [37/25/19]. Continue the game until a victor has been decided, with the Union either pushed off the board, or the Confederates stopped and can no longer advance.

Provisional Division, Army of the Tennessee
BG James B. McPherson [+1]

1st Brigade	ES	20	30	40	50	100	Status	Arm.
Col. John D. Stevenson [+1]	821	41	27	21	16	8		
1st Kansas	359	18	12	9	7	4	3	R
7th Missouri	462	23	15	12	9	5	2	R

2nd Brigade	ES	20	30	40	50	100	Status	Arm.
Col. Michael K. Lawler [+1]	817	41	27	20	16	8		
29th Illinois	429	21	14	11	9	4	3	R
31st Illinois	388	19	13	10	8	4	3	R

Author's Notes

This is a good, well-balanced game. Both sides are evenly matched. It's a large board with both open spaces and an urban town. Some works, but not enough to make it impossible or too costly to assault.

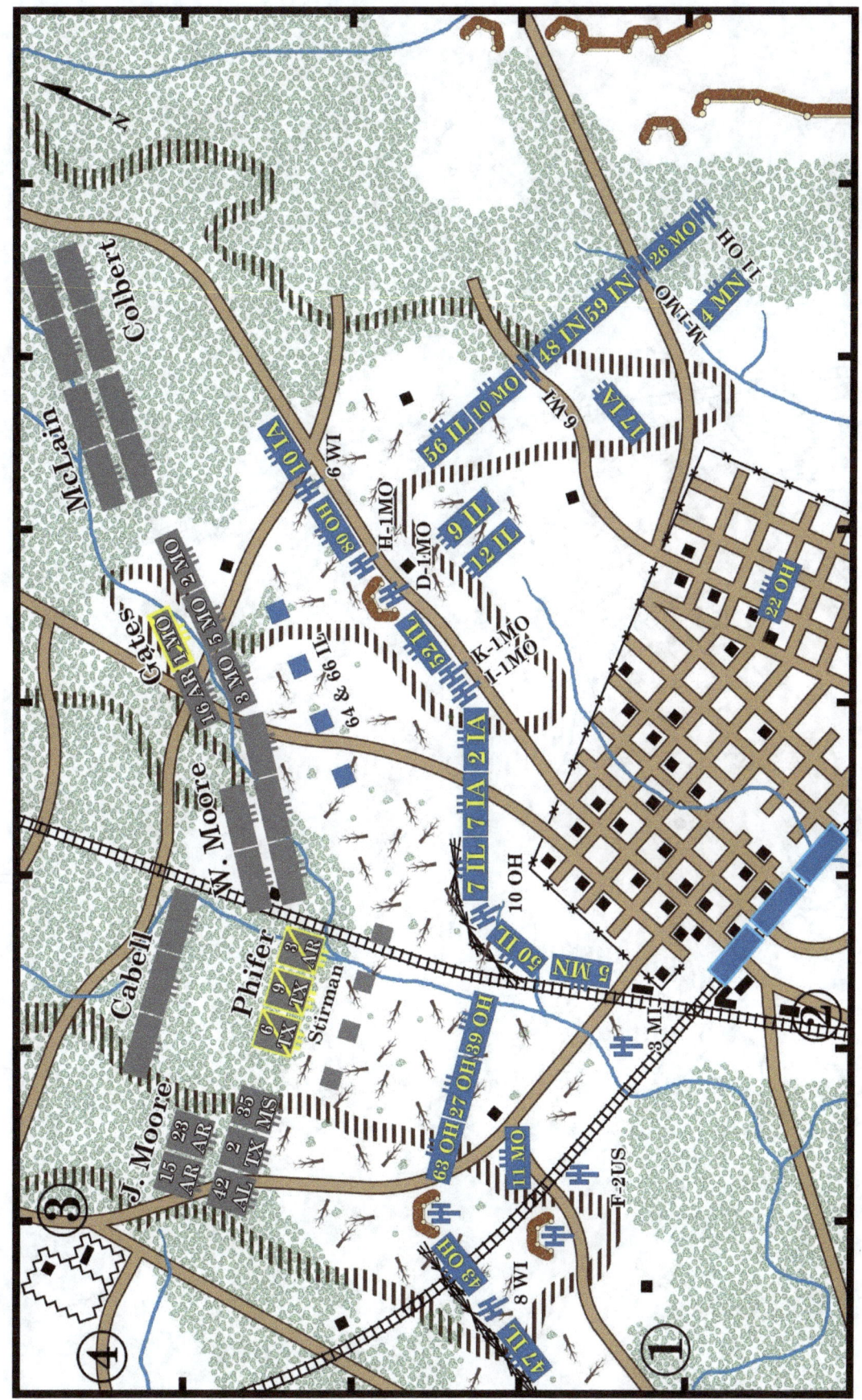

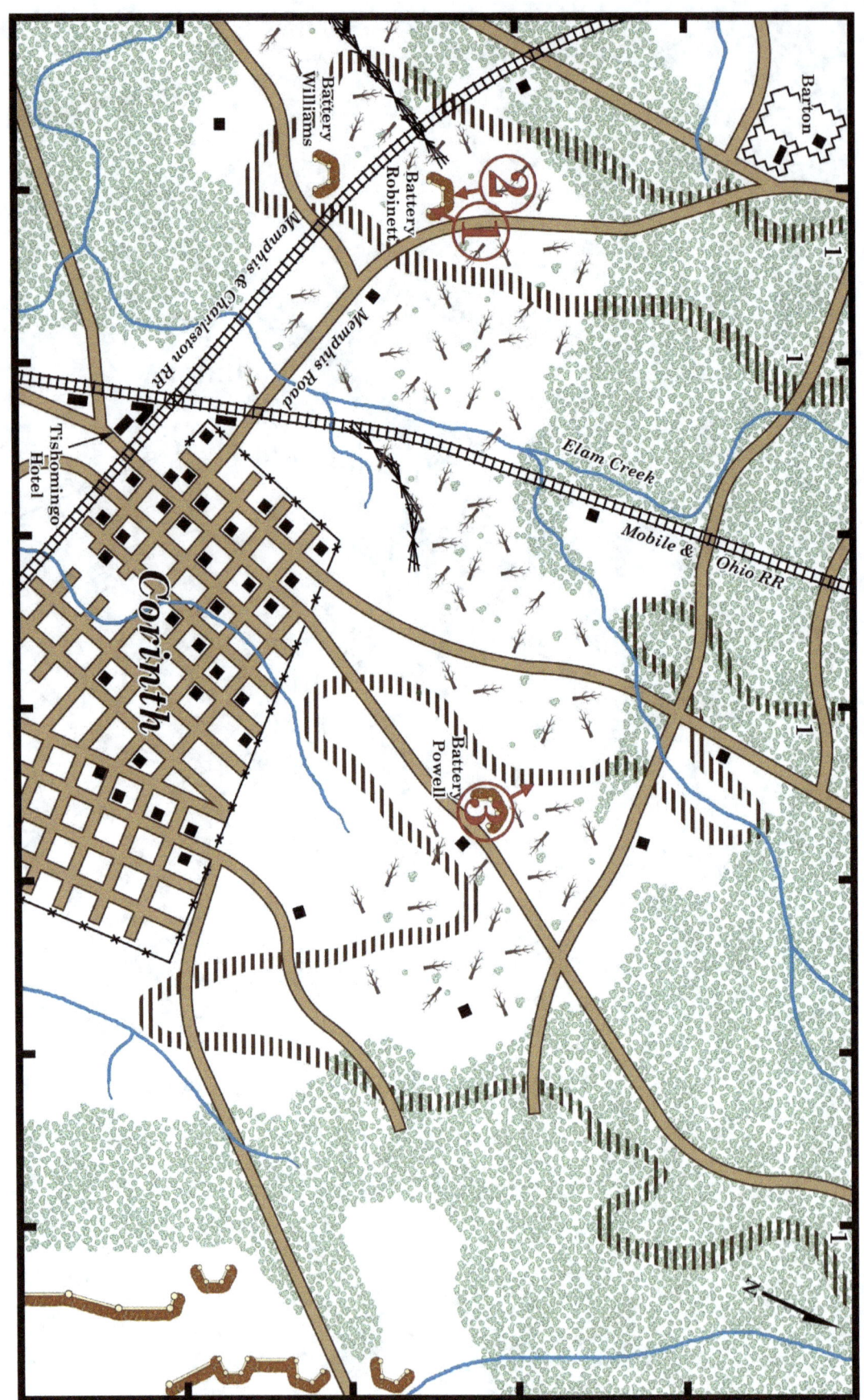

The Battle of Perryville
October 8th, 1862

Background

After abandoning Corinth in late May 1862 and assuming command of the Army of Mississippi, General Braxton Bragg spent the early summer drilling and rebuilding his army at Tupelo. In mid-July Bragg began moving his army east towards Chattanooga. Major General Edmund Kirby Smith had successfully carried out a raid into Union held Kentucky from his Department of East Tennessee, and wanted Bragg to join him in an invasion of the state. Kirby's hope was to bring the state into the Confederate cause, and recruit more soldiers into the rebel ranks. Bragg agreed, but since Smith was operating from a different department outside of his jurisdiction, he could not assume command over both until the armies joined. Bragg's army was still arriving from Tupelo, and was not ready to march into Kentucky. Smith agreed to capture Cumberland Gap, return to Chattanooga, and combine the two forces where Bragg's seniority would place him as overall commander.

Smith almost immediately reneged on the agreement. On the march, he informed Bragg that he was bypassing Cumberland Gap and heading into Kentucky. Left with no choice, Bragg began his movement north with the hopes of joining with Smith in the bluegrass state.

Word soon reached the Union army at Corinth that the Confederates had left Tupelo. Major General Don Carlos Buell marched his Army of the Ohio north to intercept. He went through Nashville, then raced north to protect Louisville on the Ohio River. At Louisville a scratch army was being raised and trained with raw recruits to confront Smith and Bragg. After small battles at Richmond and Munfordville Bragg and Buell drew near each other southeast of Louisville near Perryville.

Buell ordered his army to arrive and attack at 10 a.m. on October 8th. However, two of his three corps were delayed on the march. The fighting began in the morning, as a Union division advanced to Doctor's Creek between the line in search of scarce water, an autumn drought

Major General Alexander M. McCook

making the resource a premium. This engagement, and the difficulty in observing the enemy nestled into the rolling hills of the Kentucky countryside, deceived Bragg and his generals on the location of the Union Army. Bragg ordered Major General Leonidas Polk to attack with his corps, en echelon from right to left, with the goal of turning the Union left flank and routing the bluecoats. However, Union Major General Alexander M. McCook's I Corps lay directly astride his path, and not the open flank Bragg expected.

Major General Benjamin F. Cheatham's division opened the fight at about 2 o'clock, and ran headlong into the Federals. Brigadier General Daniel S. Donelson began the battle with an attack against what he thought was the enemy flank, but he pushed straight into the Union line and received fire from three sides. Cheatham then sent a brigade to his right to attack an open knob from where a Union battery was playing havoc with the rebels. A vicious fight ensued, spreading from north to south as more units engaged. Cheatham managed to push the Federals from two successive positions, but could not dislodge them from their third and final line as darkness descended on the battlefield.

To Cheatham's left, Brigadier General J. Patton Anderson's division attacked a strong ridge defended by Brigadier General Lovell H. Rousseau's Union division. Frontal assaults failed, but Major General Simon B. Buckner's division crossed Doctor's Creek at the

This is what Parson's Battery saw the afternoon of the battle. Maney's brigade attacked from the wood line on the small hill in the distance, and were also outflanked on the left.

Henry P. Bottom farm and outflanked the position. The Federals fell back to the high ground at the intersection of the Mackville and Benton Roads. There they held out against repeated attacks until nightfall. Reinforcements shored up the blue line just enough to prevent collapse.

McCook was left to fight on his own due to a peculiar "acoustic shadow" where atmospheric conditions prevented much of the noise of the battle from traveling southwards towards Buell and the rest of the army. They heard what they assumed was sporadic cannon fire, but did not realize McCook's entire corps was engaged. For most of the afternoon Buell and his remaining two corps were unaware that McCook was fighting for his life. Still, late afternoon advances by the II and III Corps convinced Bragg that he was heavily outnumbered. He still had not combined his army with the recalcitrant Smith, and did so at Harrodsburg. Still, logistical difficulties and the disappointing lack of the promised new Kentucky recruits forced to Bragg reluctantly retreat south, and abandon his Kentucky foray. It was the first of many retreats, no matter how justified, that would demoralize and plague the army under Bragg's command.

Bragg moved to Knoxville, then to Murfreesboro south of Nashville to threaten the important city. Buell followed, settling in Nashville later in the month. There the two armies would settle into a late autumn period of rest and reorganization until December.

Game Overview

Perryville is a large, corps-sized battle. The Confederate arrival times, while quick, are still staggered. This lends itself to a bit of a longer game, although it does give the Confederates some flexibility on where to strike. Still, this game should be played at a permanent setting, or where longer, larger games are feasible such as a gaming convention.

The game table is 5' x 8' in size. The game begins at 2:15 p.m. and ends just after nightfall on Turn [31/21/16].

Terrain

The battle occurred on the high ground between Doctor's and Wilson's Creeks. The rolling hills are common in this area of Kentucky, and plenty of high and low ground. There was a

Major General Leonidas Polk

draught in the fall of 1862, and the waterways were unusually dry. Wilson's Creek was dry, and does not affect movement. Doctor's Creek had evaporated into a series of sluggish water pools. It is easily crossed, and only deducts an inch from movement.

The elevations are ½ inch high, and cost an inch of movement to travel uphill. The woods are generally open woods, and only cost an inch to travel through. They are light woods for visibility. The wood fences and stone walls cost an inch to cross.

The cornfields do not slow movement, but they do affect visibility. Any unit inside a cornfield has visibility as if heavy woods. For units outside looking in, use the rules for looking into woods. However, visibility is not affected if the unit in the cornfield is on a slope. For example, the 38th Indiana, 10th Wisconsin, and 5th Indiana Battery on the slope of the hill in the cornfield are visible to any Confederate unit.

Deployment

Begin the game with the units set up on the board as shown. Generals Terrill and Jackson are with Parson's Battery. Rousseau and McCook are at the Russell House. Union reinforcements don't arrive for some time. Gooding's brigade arrives on the Benton Road at **1** on Turn [14/10/8]. Afterwards, Steedman's brigade arrives along the same road on Turn [17/12/9].

The Confederate en echelon attack has units entering the battle from right to left, but rather quickly. Generals Polk and Cheatham are with Donelson's brigade at the start of the battle. Maney's brigade enters at **2** on Turn [1/1/1], followed by the rest of Donelson's brigade and Carnes' Battery on Turn [2/2/2]. Brown's brigade and General Anderson enter behind Jones at **3**, and Adams at **4** on Turn [5/4/3]. General Stewart remained stationary at the beginning of the battle for lack of orders. He is released and can move freely on Turn [5/4/3]. Stanford's Battery rides on at **5** on Turn [7/5/4], as does Johnson's brigade and General Buckner at **6**. Cleburne's brigade enters at **6** on Turn [8/6/5], followed by Wood on Turn [12/8/6] and Liddell and General Hardee on Turn [14/10/8].

Victory Conditions

The battle ends if the Union are forced off the board, or the Confederates can no longer advance because of the rule's command and control guidelines. If night falls and ends the game, add up the Victory Points for enemy units eliminated. The side with the most Victory Points wins.

Order of Battle

Army of the Ohio

I Corps
MG Alexander M. McCook [+1]

Third Division
BG Lovell H. Rousseau [+2]

9th Brigade	ES	20	30	40	50	100	Status	Arm.
Col. Leonard A. Harris [+1]	2,160	108	72	54	43	22		
38th Indiana	436	22	15	11	9	4	2	R
2nd Ohio	460	23	15	12	9	5	3	R
33rd Ohio	388	19	13	10	8	4	2	R
94th Ohio	500	25	17	13	10	5	2	R
10th Wisconsin	376	19	13	9	8	4	2	M

	ES	Status	Armament		
5th Indiana Battery	90	2	**2x** 6 lb. SB, **2x** 6 lb. JR, **2x** 12 lb. H		

17th Brigade	ES	20	30	40	50	100	Status	Arm.
Col. William H. Lytle [+1]	2,469	123	82	62	49	25		
42nd Indiana	490	25	16	12	10	5	2	R
88th Indiana	434	22	14	11	9	4	2	M
15th Kentucky	517	26	17	13	10	5	2	R
3rd Ohio	500	25	17	13	10	5	3	M
10th Ohio	528	26	18	13	11	5	3	M

	ES	Status	Armament
Battery A, 1st Michigan	111	3	**6x** 10 lb. P

28th Brigade	ES	20	30	40	50	100	Status	Arm.
Col. John C. Starkweather [+1]	2,234	112	74	56	45	22		
24th Illinois	400	20	13	10	8	4	2	R
79th Pennsylvania	420	21	14	11	8	4	2	M
1st Wisconsin	407	20	14	10	8	4	2	R
21st Wisconsin	1,007	50	34	25	20	10	2	R

	ES	Status	Armament
4th Indiana Battery	140	3	**2x** 6 lb. SB, **2x** 6 lb. JR, **2x** 12 lb. H
Battery A, 1st Kentucky	140	3	**2x** 6 lb. SB, **2x** 6 lb. JR, **2x** 10 lb. P

Harris' brigade position on the ridge in the distance at the start of the battle. This is the view Jones and Brown had as they attacked across this valley. The top and slope of the ridge in the background was a cornfield during the battle.

Unattached	ES	20	30	40	50	100	Status	Arm.
2nd Kentucky Cavalry	381	19	13	10	8	4	3	BC

Tenth Division

BG James S. Jackson [+2]

33rd Brigade	ES	20	30	40	50	100	Status	Arm.
BG William R. Terrill [+1]	2,076	104	69	52	42	21		
80th Illinois	659	33	22	16	13	7	2	R
123rd Illinois	772	39	26	19	15	8	2	R
105th Ohio	645	32	22	16	13	6	2	R

	ES	Status	Armament
Parson's Independent Battery*	136	3	**5x** 12 lb. N, **2x** 12 lb. H, **1x** 10 lb. P

*Includes a section of Battery D, 1st Ohio.

34th Brigade	ES	20	30	40	50	100	Status	Arm.
Col. George P. Webster [+1]	3,029	151	101	76	61	30		
80th Indiana	738	37	25	18	15	7	2	R
50th Ohio	655	33	22	16	13	7	2	R
98th Ohio	822	41	27	21	16	8	2	R
121st Ohio	814	41	27	20	16	8	2	R

	ES	Status	Armament
19th Indiana Battery	142	2	**2x** 3" R, **4x** 12 lb. H

III Corps
First Division

3rd Brigade	ES	20	30	40	50	100	Status	Arm.
BG James B. Steedman [+1]	2,956	148	99	74	59	30		
87th Indiana	738	37	25	18	15	7	2	R
2nd Minnesota	445	22	15	11	9	4	3	R
9th Ohio	512	26	17	13	10	5	3	M
35th Ohio	615	31	21	15	12	6	3	R
18th United States	646	32	22	16	13	6	2	R

	ES	Status	Armament
Battery I, 4th United States			**4x** 12 lb. H

Ninth Division

30th Brigade	ES	20	30	40	50	100	Status	Arm.
Col. Michael Gooding [+1]	1,355	68	45	34	27	14		
59th Illinois	325	16	11	8	7	3	3	R
75th Illinois	730	37	24	18	15	7	2	R
22nd Indiana	300	15	10	8	6	3	3	R

	ES	Status	Armament
5th Wisconsin Battery	68	3	**2x** 10 lb. P, **2x** 12 lb. H, **2x** 12 lb. Mtn. H

Army of Mississippi

Right Wing
MG Leonidas Polk [+2]

First Division
MG Benjamin M. Cheatham [+2]

1st Brigade BG Daniel S. Donelson [+1]	ES	20	30	40	50	100	Status	Arm.
	1,429	71	48	36	29	14		
8th Tennessee	436	22	15	11	9	4	3	R
15th, 38th Tennessee	262	13	9	7	5	3	3	R
16th Tennessee	370	19	12	9	7	4	3	M
51st Tennessee	361	18	12	9	7	4	2	R

	ES	Status	Armament
Carnes' Tennessee Battery		3	**4x** 6 lb. SB

2nd Brigade BG Alexander P. Stewart [+1]	ES	20	30	40	50	100	Status	Arm.
	1,466	73	49	37	29	15		
4th, 5th Tennessee	457	23	15	11	9	5	3	M
24th Tennessee	375	19	13	9	8	4	3	R
31st Tennessee	324	16	11	8	6	3	3	M
33rd Tennessee	310	16	10	8	6	3	3	R

	ES	Status	Armament
Stanford's Mississippi Battery	112	3	**4x** 3" R

3rd Brigade BG George E. Maney [+1]	ES	20	30	40	50	100	Status	Arm.
	1,822	91	61	46	36	18		
41st Georgia	520	26	17	13	10	5	2	M
1st Tennessee	400	20	13	10	8	4	3	R
6th, 27th Tennessee	524	26	17	13	10	5	3	R
9th Tennessee	378	19	13	9	8	4	3	M

	ES	Status	Armament
Turner's Mississippi Battery	105	3	**2x** 6 lb. SB, **2x** 12 lb. H

Cavalry Brigade Col. John A. Wharton [+1]	ES	20	30	40	50	100	Status	Arm.
	800	40	27	20	16	8		
2nd Georgia Cavalry*	386	19	13	10	8	4	3	Sh
8th Texas Cavalry	414	21	14	10	8	4	4	C

*Includes 1st Kentucky, 4th Kentucky, and Davis' Tennessee Cavalry Bn.

Looking down on the Henry "Squire" Botton farm from the Union position on the ridge above. The house is still standing, but is obscured by the trees on the right of the road. The barn and small cornfield would have been in the open area to the right. The ford across Doctor's Creek is at the bottom of the hill.

Left Wing
MG William J. Hardee [+2]

Second Division
BG J. Patton Anderson [+2]

1st Brigade	ES	20	30	40	50	100	Status	Arm.
BG John C. Brown [+1]	977	49	33	24	20	10		
1st Florida	303	15	10	8	6	3	3	R
3rd Florida	247	12	8	6	5	2	2	R
41st Mississippi	427	21	14	11	9	4	2	M

	ES	Status	Armament
Battery A, 14th Georgia	125	3	**3x** 6 lb. SB, **3x** 12 lb. H

2nd Brigade	ES	20	30	40	50	100	Status	Arm.
BG Daniel W. Adams [+1]	1,770	89	59	44	35	18		
13th Louisiana	328	16	11	8	7	3	3	M
16th Louisiana	422	21	14	11	8	4	3	M
20th Louisiana	360	18	12	9	7	4	3	R
25th Louisiana	510	26	17	13	10	5	3	R
14th Louisiana Sharpshooter Bn.	150	8	5	4	3	2	3	R
	ES	Status	Armament					
Slocumb's Louisiana Battery*	150	3	2x 6 lb. SB, 2x 3" R, 2x 12 lb. H					

*5th Company, Washington Artillery

4th Brigade	ES	20	30	40	50	100	Status	Arm.
Col. Thomas M. Jones [+1]	1,012	51	34	25	20	10		
27th Mississippi	350	18	12	9	7	4	2	R
30th Mississippi	362	18	12	9	7	4	2	M
34th Mississippi	300	15	10	8	6	3	2	M
	ES	Status	Armament					
Lumsden's Alabama Battery	125	3	4x 12 lb. N					

Third Division

MG Simon B. Buckner [+2]

1st Brigade	ES	20	30	40	50	100	Status	Arm.
BG St. John R. Liddell [+1]	1,683	84	56	42	34	17		
2nd Arkansas	416	21	14	10	8	4	3	R
5th, 7th Arkansas	577	29	19	14	12	6	3	M
6th Arkansas	362	18	12	9	7	4	3	R
8th Arkansas	328	16	11	8	7	3	4	M
	ES	Status	Armament					
Swett's Mississippi Battery	70	3	6x 6 lb. SB, 2x 12 lb. H					

2nd Brigade	ES	20	30	40	50	100	Status	Arm.
BG Patrick R. Cleburne [+1]	900	45	30	23	18	9		
13th & 15th Arkansas, 2nd TN	380	19	13	10	8	4	4	R
35th, 48th Tennessee	520	26	17	13	10	5	3	R
	ES	Status	Armament					
Calvert's Arkansas Battery		3	2x 6 lb. SB, 2x 12 lb. H					

3rd Brigade	ES	20	30	40	50	100	Status	Arm.
Bushrod R. Johnson [+1]	1,475	74	49	37	30	15		
5th Confederate	240	12	8	6	5	2	3	R
17th, 37th Tennessee	430	22	14	11	9	4	3	M
23rd, 44th Tennessee	430	22	14	11	9	4	3	M
25th Tennessee	375	19	13	9	8	4	3	R

	ES	Status	Armament
Darden's Mississippi Battery	65	3	**2x** 6 lb. SB, **2x** 12 lb. H

4th Brigade	ES	20	30	40	50	100	Status	Arm.
BG Sterling A. M. Wood [+1]	1,031	52	34	26	21	10		
33rd Alabama	380	19	13	10	8	4	2	R
15th Mississippi Sharpshooter Bn.	57	3	2	1	1	1	3	R
32nd, 45th Mississippi	594	30	20	15	12	6	2	M

	ES	Status	Armament
Semple's Alabama Battery	109	3	**4x** 12 lb. N, **2x** 6 lb. JR

Optional Rules

There are no optional rules for this game, although you could release Stewart's brigade at the start of the battle instead of having it idle for the first few turns.

Author's Notes

Perryville is a straight up fight, and a near perfect wargame. The Union lines are set, but the Confederates get a little bit of maneuver room and choices as their divisions march on the board. Do they reinforce Cheatham, or continue into the Union position above the Bottoms house. Can Cheatham hold them in place, or will the Rousseau be able to send units from his left to right to stem the rebel tide?

The modern battlefield is also a model of reclamation and preservation. I highly recommend visiting it if you get the chance.

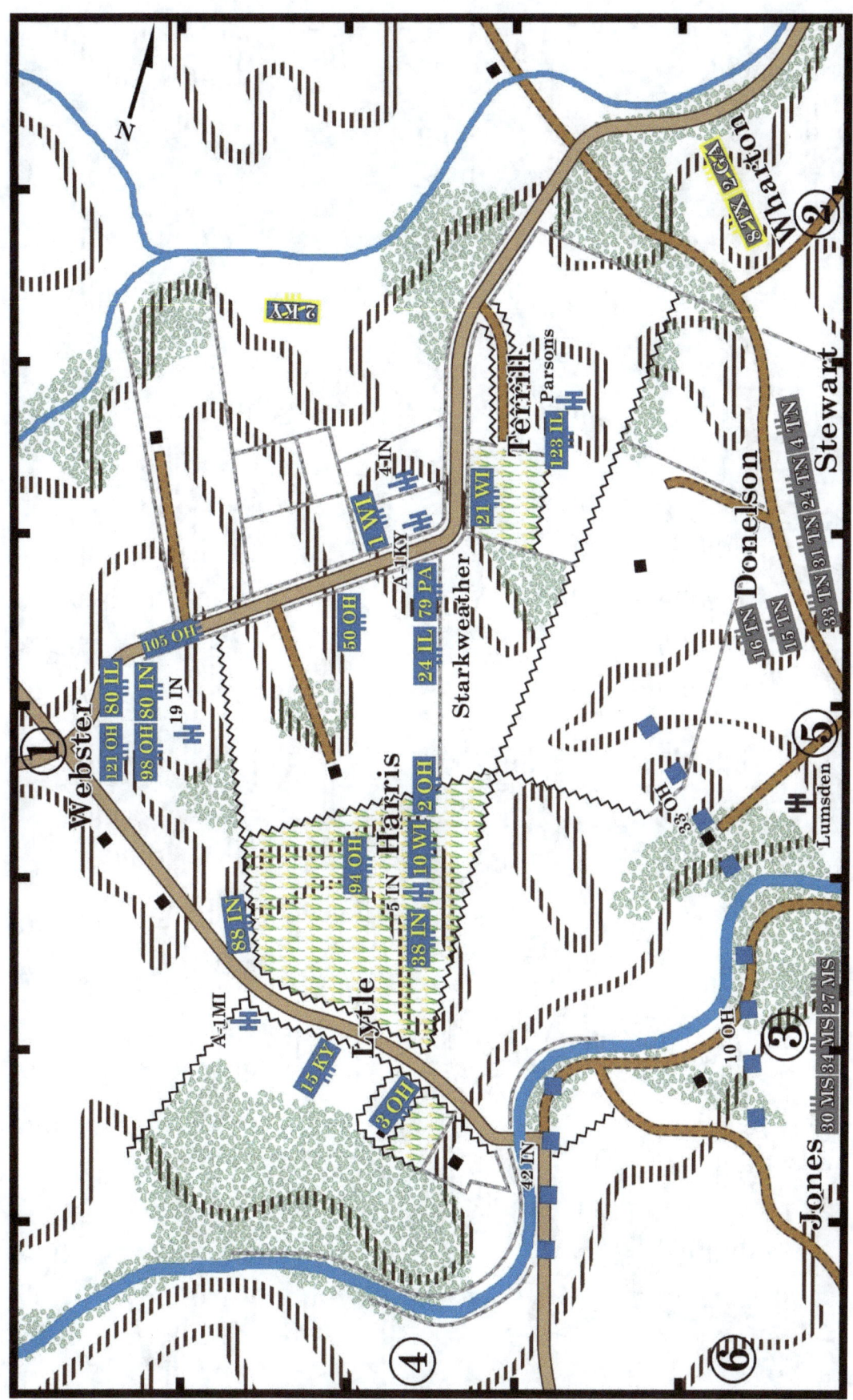

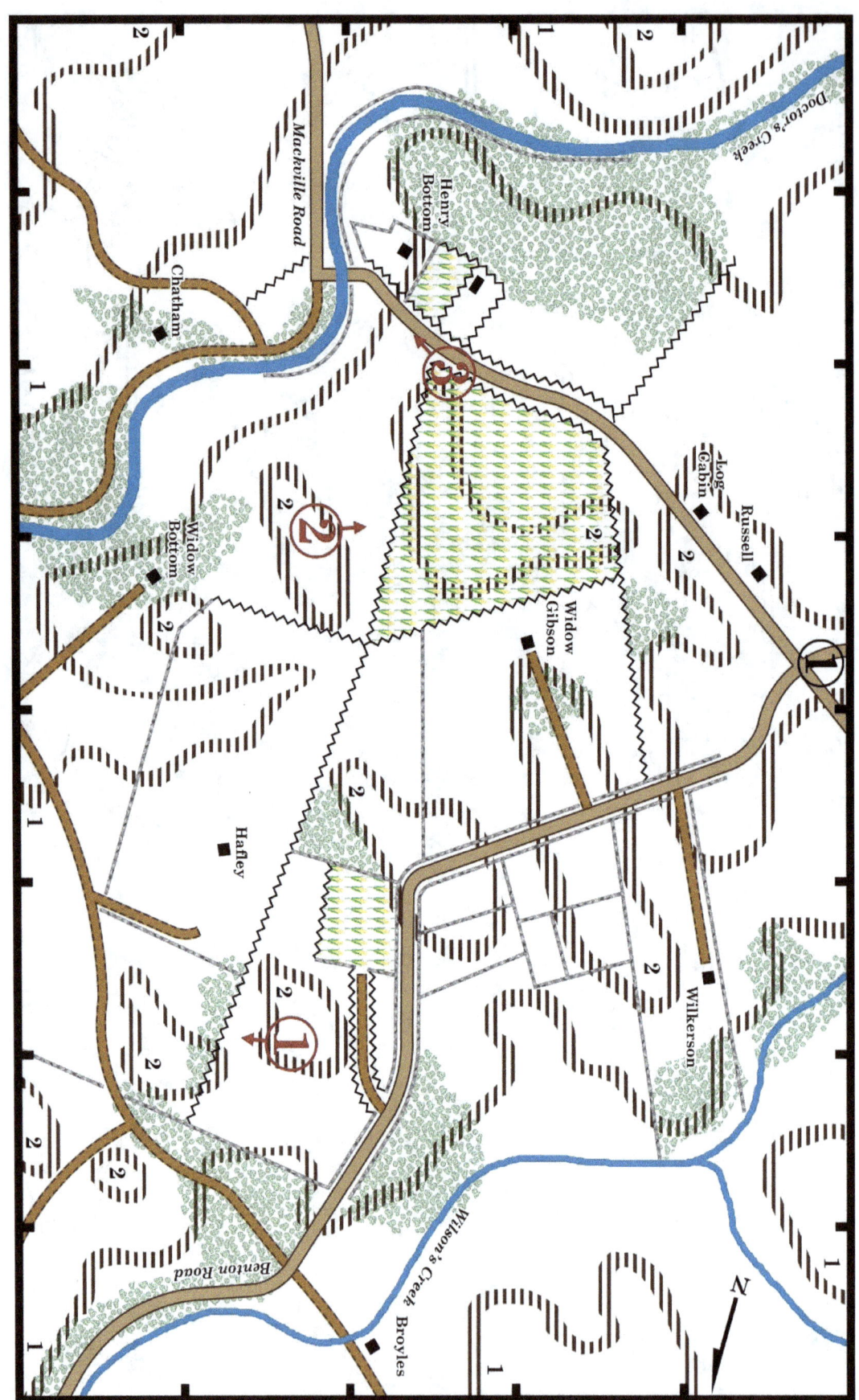

The Battle of Stones River: Opening
December 31st, 1862

Background

After the Kentucky Campaign the two opposing armies settled into their camps in middle Tennessee: The Union at Nashville and the Confederates at Murfreesboro, 30 miles to the southeast. The Lincoln administration relieved Don Carlos Buell from the command of the Army of the Ohio for lack of energy and initiative, and replaced him with Major General William S. Rosecrans, recent victor of Iuka and Corinth. Rosecrans renamed it the Army of the Cumberland as the department it operated from encompassed much of the area of the Cumberland River, including Nashville. The army contained three "corps", a left, center, and right wing, but officially the entire army was the Fourteenth Army Corps. It would be designated with proper corps numbers the next year. Rosecrans spent November and December rebuilding and training his army, with Washington breathing down his neck to move on Braxton Bragg's army at Murfreesboro. This only intensified after the Union defeat at Fredericksburg in mid-December.

Bragg had problems of his own. He spent the same time period much as Rosecrans did, rebuilding and reorganizing his army. After combining his Army of the Mississippi with E. Kirby Smith's Army of Kentucky, he renamed it the Army of Tennessee, which it would fight under for the remainder of the war. Jefferson Davis' Confederate government also pressured Bragg for action. With Grant pushing hard in northern Mississippi towards Vicksburg, Davis ordered Bragg to detach a division and send it to reinforce the beleaguered fortress city. They would be sorely missed in the coming weeks.

On December 26th Rosecrans made his move. He sent his three wings on separate but supporting roads to the southeast towards Murfreesboro. Confederate cavalry blocked and harassed him the entire way. He arrived opposite the town on the 29th. The Union spent much of the 30th skirmishing and slowly moving forward

Brigadier General Richard W. Johnson

into close contact with the Confederate defensive line. As darkness fell the two lines were only 700 yards apart.

Rosecrans' plan for the next day was to attack on his left, seizing the high ground across Stones River, from which vantage point his artillery could dominate the Confederate defenses. Major General Alexander McCook, who held the flank at Perryville that was almost overrun, was tasked by Rosecrans to hold out against any attack for a few hours until the Confederate flank had been turn. Ironically, Bragg's plan was the same. He heavily reinforced his left (the Union right) and intended to roll up the Union line, capture the Nashville Turnpike and parallel Nashville & Chattanooga Railroad, and cut Rosecrans off from Nashville. The winner would likely be the army that struck first.

That army was Bragg's. At 6 a.m. Major General John P. McCown's division jumped off, with Major General Patrick R. Cleburne's division in close support behind it. Brigadier General Richard W. Johnson's Union division received the first blow. Johnson's men had not had time to adequately reconnoiter the ground the previous evening, as they only arrived in position at dusk. Although skirmish lines were well posted and gave warning of the attack, the speed and ferocity of the oncoming grey warriors overwhelmed the defenders. Brigadier General Edward N. Kirk's brigade was in formation and ready, but the rebels quickly overran them. Many

The modern view of the opening of the battle. The intersection with the street lights is the Franklin Road, stretching to the distance, and Gresham Lane, to the right. The square woodlot to the west of Gresham Lane was located where the light tan building is today.

of Brigadier General August Willich's brigade, holding the flank, were cooking breakfast and not in formation. The two Union batteries present had sent half their horses to nearby Puckett Creek to water them, limiting their mobility. Kirk was seriously wounded, Willich was captured, and the Union flank collapsed. Once again on the receiving end of a Confederate assault, McCook's flank crumbled.

The Confederates continued north. Colonels P. Sidney Post and Philemon P. Baldwin's brigades shifted to meet the oncoming Confederate attack, now moving north following Gresham Lane. Despite desperate stands and inflicting severe casualties on the attackers, first Post, and then Baldwin, were swept away by the grey tide. By 9 o'clock the remnants of Johnson's division were in headlong flight to the Wilkinson Turnpike to the north. Rosecrans would have his hands full salvaging a victory from the day's fighting.

Game Overview

This scenario is a mid-sized fight pitting 4 brigades on the defensive verses 6 attacking brigades. The Confederates have the early advantage of surprise, but terrain still favors the defenders, even if they do begin at a disadvantage.

The table size is 4' x 6'. The game begins as the sky brightens at 6:15 a.m., and ends at 9:00 a.m. on Turn [17/12/9].

Terrain

The game map is flat, but cut with fenced in fields and woodlots. The fences cost an inch of movement to cross, as does Puckett Creek. There are two types of forest present on the map. The brown winter woods are generally open. They only deduct an inch from open movement, and visibility is for light woods. The green woods are cedar breaks and limestone outcroppings. Movement through these woods is broken terrain, or one full terrain type worse than open. Visibility is for heavy woods. In addition, the thicker woods and rocks provide an additional cover bonus, though it should be the smallest cover advantage available and not overwhelming.

Many of cornfields in the area were left standing during the winter. Those specifically marked as cornfields do not affect movement, but visibility in them is the same as light woods. Most of the open fields on the map were cornfields too, but had been harvested and only stalks remained.

Major General Patrick R. Cleburne

A light fog covered the ground during the opening of the battle, and helped the Confederates get close to the Union lines without detection. Until the end of Turn [4/3/2] all visibility is restricted to the same as light woods. Units can still fire, of course, but most rules have allowances for area or blind fire in these types of situations where the two units cannot see each other.

The first turns are also fought in the morning twilight. The fog covers most of the same visibility restrictions, so there is no need to duplicate the effects. However, until daylight at the beginning of Turn [5/4/3] all firing strengths are halved. This is also the same turn all the fog effects are removed, so Turn [5/4/3] begins with no visibility restrictions.

Deployment

Begin the game set up as shown on the scenario map. For the Union, the 15th Ohio and 89th Illinois of Willich's brigade are in camp and in disorder. Baldwin's brigade is likewise in disorder at the top of the map. All of the Union batteries are unlimbered. General Kirk is with the 34th Illinois, while Generals Johnson and Willich are at Johnson's headquarters near Baldwin's brigade.

The advance of the Confederates came as a surprise to the Union defenders. Kirk and Post's brigades are in formation and were ready before dawn. Still, the Confederates struck hard and fast, aided by the corn and the morning fog. Kirk ordered the 34th Indiana to charge to stall the Confederates, so the Hoosiers *must* be ordered to charge the first turn. The 79th Illinois from the brigade was to the north guarding wagons. The colonel immediately marched to the sound of the guns. The regiment enters at **1** on Turn [12/8/6]. They can be in any formation.

The 32nd and 39th Indiana in Willich's brigade had most of the regiments either on the skirmish line, or in reserve along the Franklin Road. The 15th Ohio and 89th Illinois were still in camp. These two regiments may not move or be given orders for Turn [1/1/1]. They are released normally beginning Turn [2/2/2].

Baldwin's brigade may not move or be given orders until Turn [5/4/3].

About half of the horses from Batteries A and E, 1st Ohio were watering at Puckett Creek. Until the horses return, the batteries take double the time to limber and unlimber, and move at half speed. The horses return on Turn [5/4/3] regardless of where the batteries are located (no need to overly complicate things).

The Confederate attack is pretty straightforward. McCown's Division is in the lead, followed by Cleburne's. All Confederate units on the board *must* be given a forward order on the first turn, either move or charge. They may not remain stationary. McCown is behind Ector's Brigade.

The rest of Cleburne's Division enters immediately as space allows. Johnson's Brigade marches onto the board at **2** in line of battle on Turn [4/3/2]. From left to right, the brigade is aligned as: 23rd, 17th, 25th, and 44th Tennessee. Darden's Battery is behind the center of the brigade, and Cleburne is with them. Polk's Brigade marches onto the board in line of battle at **3** on Turn [5/4/3]. From left to right they are: 5th Tennessee, 1st Arkansas, 2nd Tennessee, and 13th & 15th Arkansas. Key's Battery is behind the center of the brigade. The rest of McCown's artillery, Douglas and Humprey's batteries, along with General Hardee, enter limbered on the Franklin Road at **3** on Turn [7/5/4]. Finally, Wharton's cavalry brigade marches onto the board at **4** on Turn [8/6/5].

Victory Conditions

The game ends at 9 a.m. on Turn [17/12/9]. The objective of the Confederates is to turn the flank and force the Union off the board. The Union objective is to keep their brigades intact.

At the end of the game, add up the Victory Points for enemy units eliminated. The side with the most points wins.

Order of Battle

Army of the Cumberland (Fourteenth Corps)

Right Wing
First Division

1st Brigade Col. P. Sidney Post [+1]	ES	20	30	40	50	100	Status	Arm.
	1,418	65	43	32	26	13		
59th Illinois	298	15	10	7	6	3	3	R
74th Illinois	341	17	11	9	7	3	3	R
75th Illinois	353	18	12	9	7	4	2	R
22nd Indiana	306	15	10	8	6	3	3	R

	ES	Status	Armament
5th Wisconsin Battery	120	3	**2x** 10 lb. P, **2x** 12 lb. H, **2x** 12 lb. H

Second Division
BG Richard W. Johnson [+2]

1st Brigade BG August Willich [+1]	ES	20	30	40	50	100	Status	Arm.
	1,650	76	51	38	31	15		
89th Illinois	311	16	10	8	6	3	2	R
32nd Indiana, 49th Ohio	513	26	17	13	10	5	3	R
39th Indiana	395	20	13	10	8	4	3	R
15th Ohio	309	15	10	8	6	3	3	R

	ES	Status	Armament
Battery A, 1st Ohio	122	3	**2x** 6 lb. SB, **2x** 6 lb. JR, **2x** 12 lb. H

2nd Brigade BG Edward N. Kirk [+1]	ES	20	30	40	50	100	Status	Arm.
	2,042	96	64	48	38	19		
34th Illinois	354	18	12	9	7	4	3	R
79th Illinois	437	22	15	11	9	4	3	R
29th Indiana	337	17	11	8	7	3	3	R
30th Indiana	487	24	16	12	10	5	3	R
77th Pennsylvania	307	15	10	8	6	3	3	R

	ES	Status	Armament
Battery E, 1st Ohio	120		**5x** 6 lb. JR, **1x** 6 lb. SB

Looking north down Gresham Lane from the Franklin Road intersection.

3rd Brigade Col. Philemon P. Baldwin [+1]	ES	20	30	40	50	100	Status	Arm.
	2,232	106	70	53	42	21		
6th Indiana	451	23	15	11	9	5	3	R
5th Kentucky	524	26	17	13	10	5	3	R
1st Ohio	487	24	16	12	10	5	3	R
93rd Ohio	652	33	22	16	13	7	2	R
	ES	Status	Armament					
5th Indiana Battery	118	3	2x 10 lb. P, 2x 6 lb. JR, 2x 12 lb. N					

Army of Tennessee

Hardee's Corps
LG William J. Hardee [+2]

Cleburne's Division
MG Patrick R. Cleburne [+3]

1st Brigade BG Lucius E. Polk [+1]	ES	20	30	40	50	100	Status	Arm.
	1,745	83	56	42	33	17		
1st Arkansas	400	20	13	10	8	4	4	R
13th & 15th Arkansas	375	19	13	9	8	4	3	R
5th Tennessee, 5th Confederate	520	26	17	13	10	5	3	R
2nd Tennessee	370	19	12	9	7	4	4	R

	ES	Status	Armament				
Key's Arkansas Battery	80	3	2x 6 lb. SB; 2x 12 lb. H				

2nd Brigade	ES	20	30	40	50	100	Status	Arm.
BG S. John R. Liddell [+1]	1,276	64	43	32	26	13		
2nd Arkansas	300	15	10	8	6	3	3	R
5th Arkansas	336	17	11	8	7	3	3	R
6th & 7th Arkansas	370	19	12	9	7	4	4	R
8th Arkansas	270	14	9	7	5	3	4	M

	ES	Status	Armament
Warren Mississippi Battery		3	4x 6 lb. SB, 2x 12 lb. H

3rd Brigade	ES	20	30	40	50	100	Status	Arm.
BG Bushrod R. Johnson [+1]	2,010	97	65	49	39	19		
17th Tennessee	598	30	20	15	12	6	4	R
23rd, 37th Tennessee	497	25	17	12	10	5	4	R
25th Tennessee	336	17	11	8	7	3	3	R
44th Tennessee	509	25	17	13	10	5	4	M

	ES	Status	Armament
Darden's Mississippi Battery	70	3	2x 6 lb. SB, 2x 12 lb. H

McCown's Division
MG John P. McCown [+2]

1st Brigade	ES	20	30	40	50	100	Status	Arm.
BG Mathew D. Ector [+1]	1,440	72	48	36	29	14		
10th Texas Cavalry (Dismounted)	400	20	13	10	8	4	3	M
11th Texas Cavalry (Dismounted)	370	19	12	9	7	4	3	R
14th Texas Cavalry (Dismounted)	300	15	10	8	6	3	3	M
32nd Texas Cavalry (Dismounted)	370	19	12	9	7	4	3	R

	ES	Status	Armament
Douglas' Texas Battery	90	3	2x 6 lb. SB, 2x 12 lb. H

2nd Brigade	ES	20	30	40	50	100	Status	Arm.
BG James E. Rains [+1]	1,260	63	42	32	25	13		
3rd Georgia Bn.	300	15	10	8	6	3	3	R
9th Georgia Bn.	260	13	9	7	5	3	3	M
29th North Carolina	300	15	10	8	6	3	3	R
11th Tennessee	400	20	13	10	8	4	3	M

3rd Brigade	ES	20	30	40	50	100	Status	Arm.
BG Evander McNair [+1]	1,376	69	46	34	28	14		
1st Arkansas Mounted Rifles	370	19	12	9	7	4	3	R
2nd Arkansas Mounted Rifles, 30th AR	536	27	18	13	11	5	3	R
4th Arkansas, 4th Arkansas Bn.	470	24	16	12	9	5	3	R

	ES	Status	Armament					
Humphrey's Arkansas Battery	120	3	2x 6 lb. SB, 2x 12 lb. H					

Cavalry Brigade	ES	20	30	40	50	100	Status	Arm.
BG John A. Wharton [+1]	770	39	26	19	15	8		
8th Texas Cavalry[1]	400	20	13	10	8	4	3	M
1st Confederate Cavalry[2]	370	19	12	9	7	4	3	R

[1]Includes the 2nd Georgia and 3rd Confederate Cavalry.

[2]Includes Murray's Tennessee, 14th Alabama, and Davis' Tennessee Cavalry battalions.

Optional Rules

There can be a mix of optional rules for this game, most of which relate to releasing held units early. So, Willich's brigade can all move on the first turn, or likewise with Baldwin. Or the Confederates are free to do anything on the first turn instead of moving forward, while the 34th Illinois can hold fast.

Also included is a larger 5' x 8' map. It might be a bit of an overkill for this size battle, but it will allow the Union player to have more space to fall back, rally, and resist the Confederate onslaught. Honestly, it's probably more historically accurate, but more work to set up. If using the larger map, the 79th Illinois enters at **1** on Turn [10/7/5].

Author's Notes

This game is a short, sharp fight. The Confederates need to hit the Union fast and hard. No time for fancy maneuvering if they want to inflict as many casualties as they can before the deadline. Just forge straight ahead and charge! On the other hand, the Union have to play it smart. It will take skill to form defensive lines after the initial shock of the assault wears off, and the Confederates still have the numerical advantage. If you are a defensive-minded player, this game is the challenge you have been looking for.

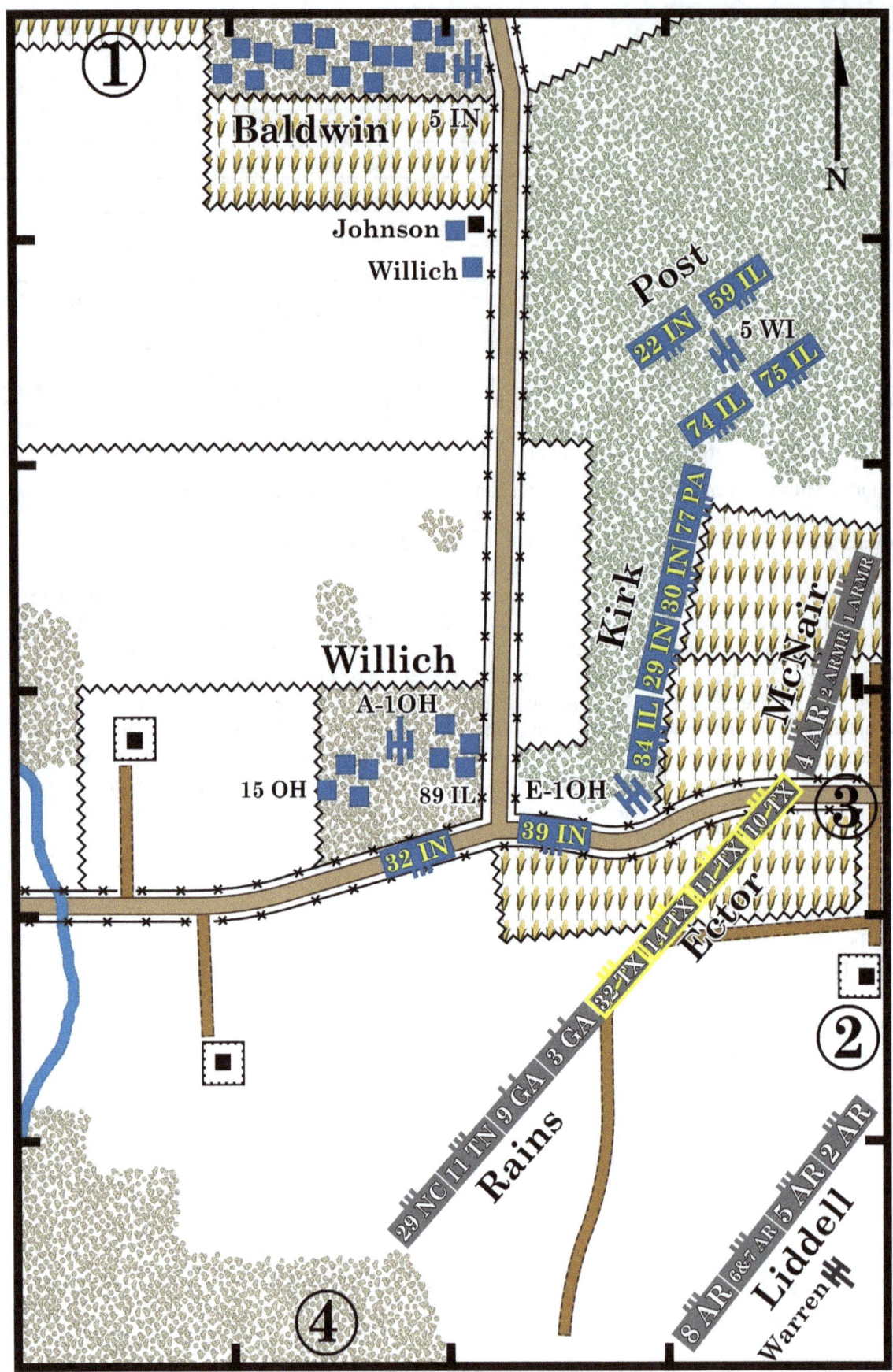

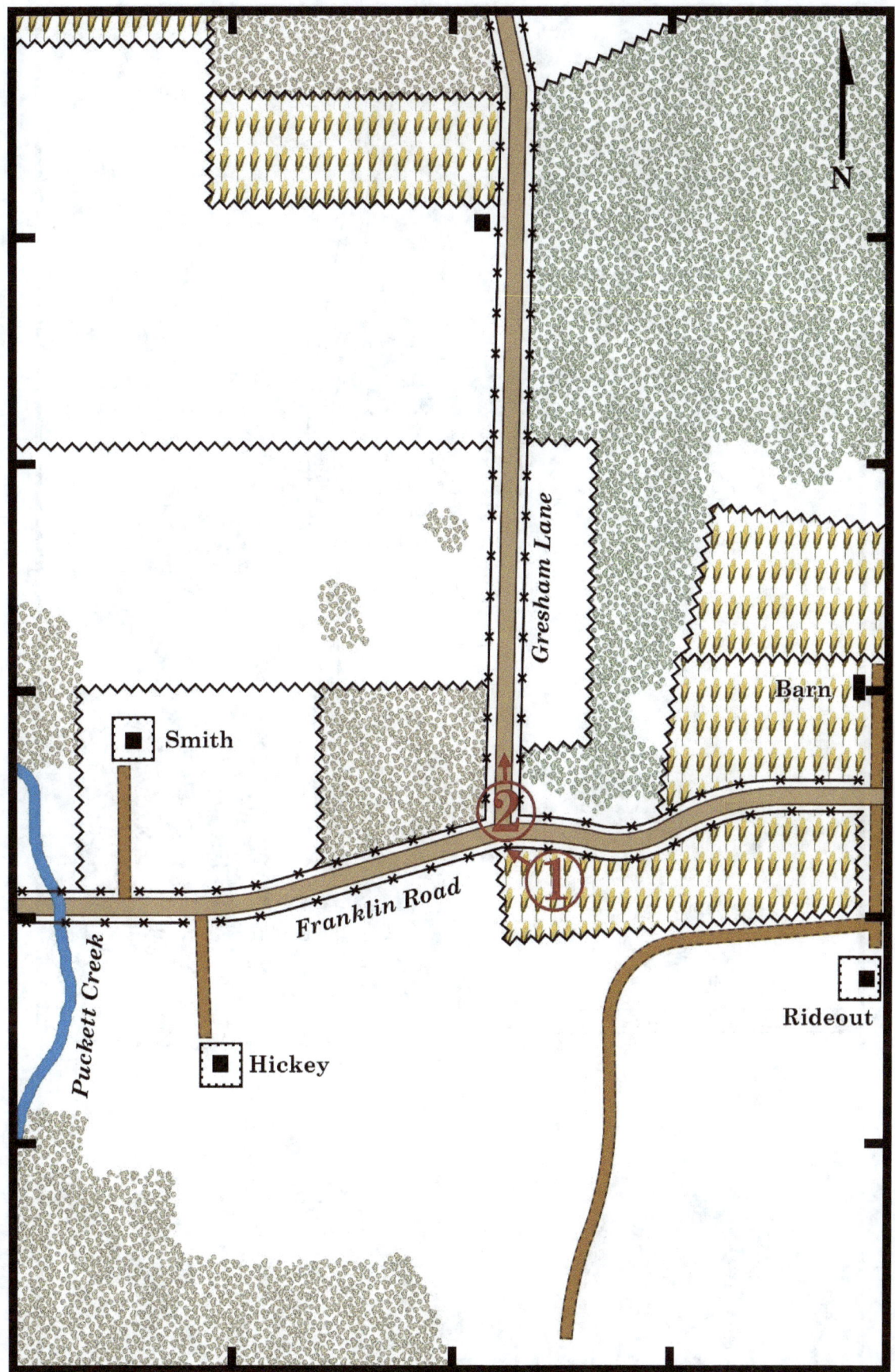

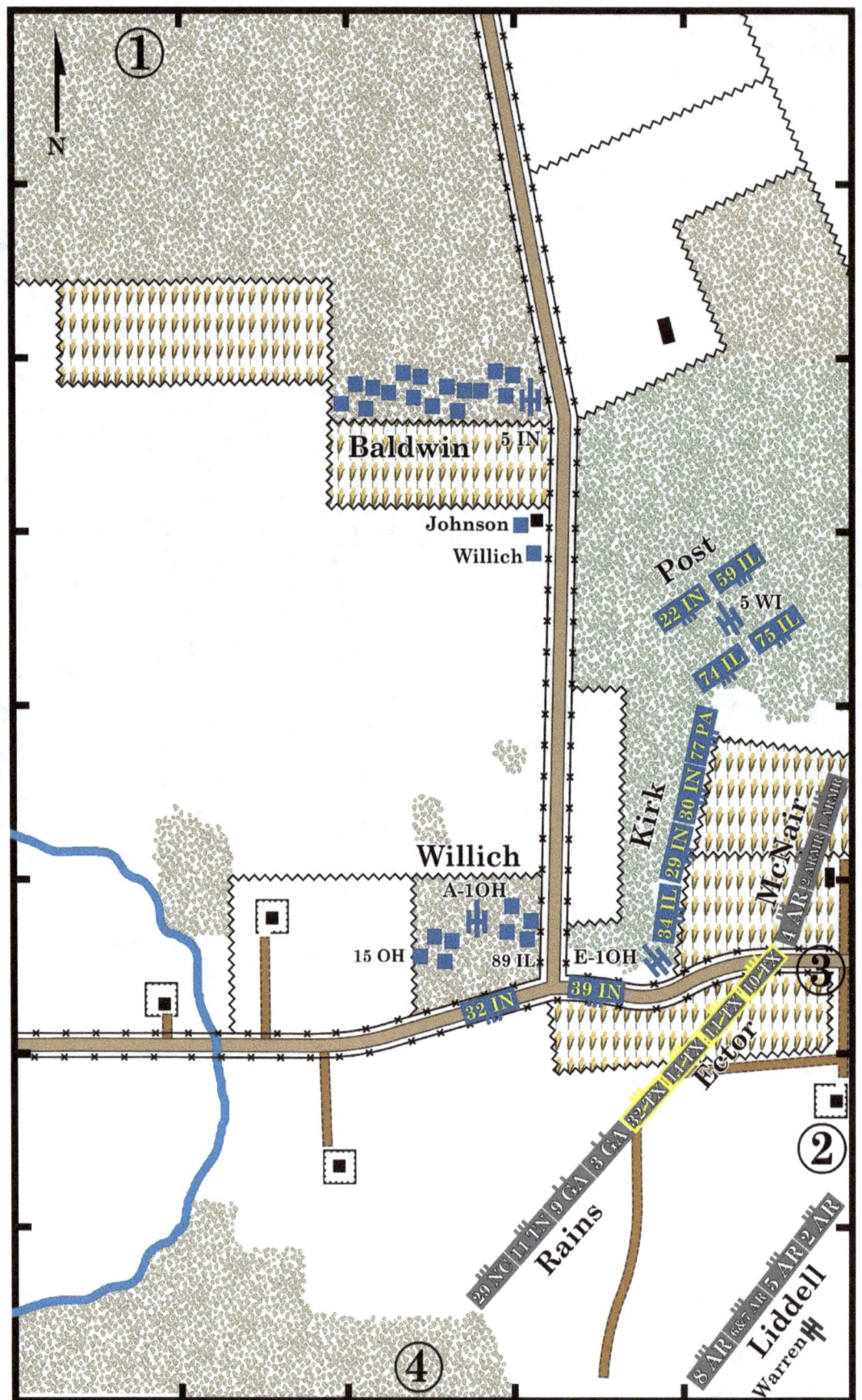

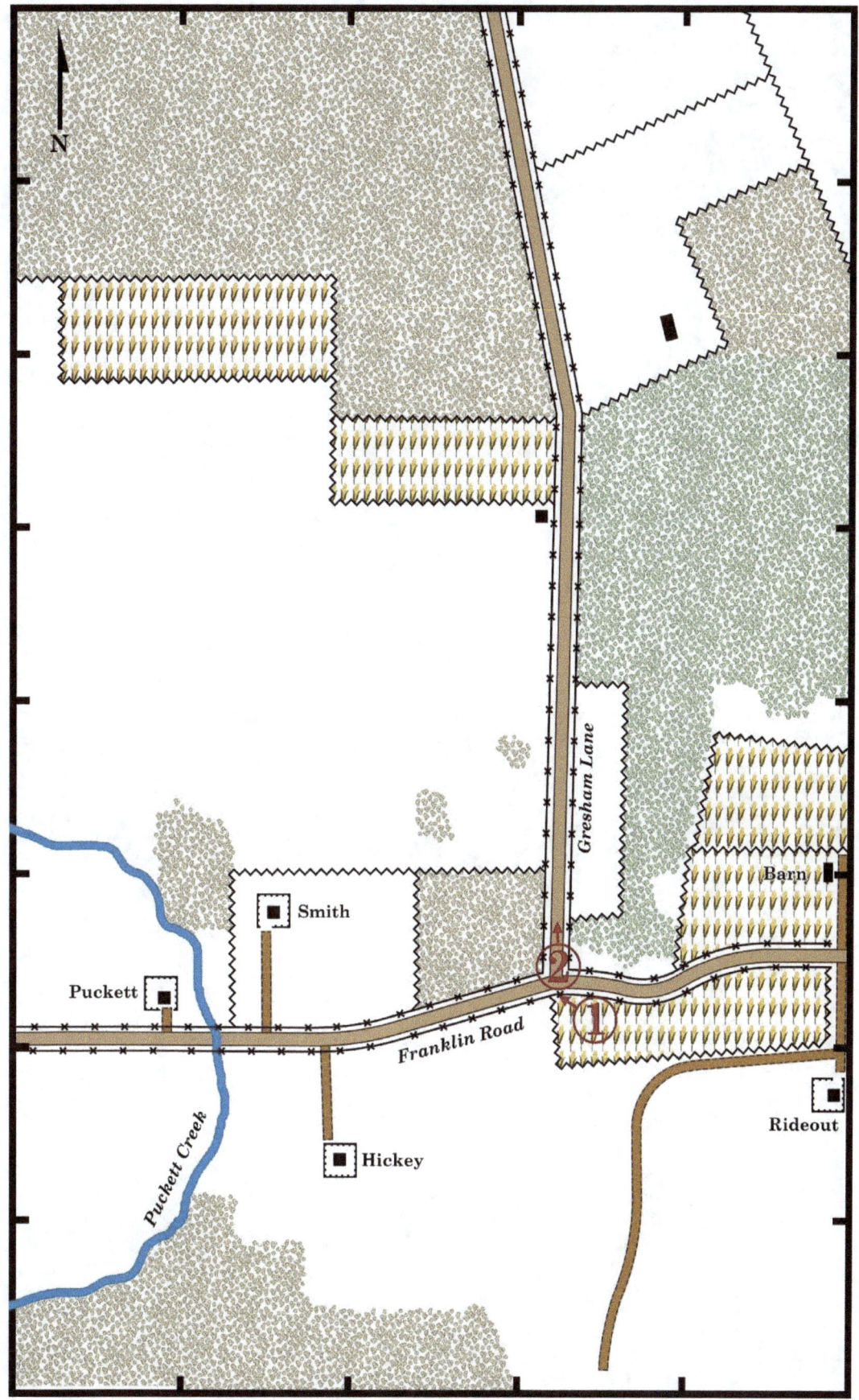

The Battle of Stones River: Sheridan Holds the Line
December 31st, 1862

Background

The Battle of Stones River began at 6:22 a.m. according to Brigadier General August Willich's watch, and by 7 o'clock his brigade and most of his parent division were in full retreat. This collapse exposed the flank of the next division in the Union line, commanded by Brigadier General Jefferson C. Davis. Already one of Davis' brigades was streaming back in flight.

Major General Alexander M. McCook was expected to hold the right flank of the Union army while the left launched a decisive attack against the Confederate right. With two of his three divisions out of the fight within an hour, the prospects of achieving that directive seemed grim. Anchoring McCook's left on the Wilkinson Turnpike, and tying in with the Center Wing, was Brigadier General Philip H. Sheridan with his last division.

The Confederates kept up a steady pressure with their en echelon attack, with the fighting spreading from south to north as each rebel brigade stepped off in succession. The fighting men attacking McCook here were from Lieutenant General Leonidas Polk's corps. Like Hardee to their left, the corps' two divisions were stacked one behind the other. Major General Jones M. Withers led the front, while Major General Benjamin F. Cheatham followed with his supporting division.

The Confederates crashed into Davis like a gale force wind. The Federals enjoyed some success repulsing the first Confederate brigade, but gradually units from Major General Patrick R. Cleburne's division moved around the Union flank through the dense cedar forest. Davis was eventually forced back.

Sheridan fought tenaciously around the Giles Harding farm in a whirlwind of chaos. All three of his brigade commanders perished in the maelstrom. The Confederates fed brigade after brigade into the melee, including a charge Cheatham led personally. As the fighting spread

Brigadier General Philip H. Sheridan

north of the Wilkinson pike, Sheridan was eventually forced back. Still, his stand and sacrificed bought time for General Rosecrans to call off his planned offensive and hurry those units to the south to stem the Confederate tide.

The day's fighting would end with the Union army barely holding onto the Nashville Road, with the rebels having pushed them back almost three and a half miles. The next day the two armies would rest, but on New Year's Day General Bragg would launch an offensive on the northern end of the line. It would end in failure, and two days later Bragg, fearing Union reinforcements would outnumber his army, began his retreat south to Tullahoma, ending the short winter campaign. It was a Union victory, but an extremely costly one.

Game Overview

This is a corps-sized game with the Confederates trying to push the Union off the board in their continuing attack at Stones River. If McCook and his corps can delay the Confederates until 11 o'clock, it will materially aid Rosecrans by allowing him to pull divisions off the line to the north and rush them south to defeat the Confederate attack.

The game map is 4' x 6' in size. The game begins at 7:00 a.m. and ends at 10:00 a.m. on Turn [25/17/13].

Terrain

Like most of this area of the battlefield, the real-life elevations are slight and barely perceptible. The dominating features are the forest and farm fences. The fences cost an inch to cross, as does the small stream. There are two types of woods. The brown winter woods are open, and only deduct an inch from open movement. They are light woods for visibility. The green woods are heavy with cedars and limestone outcroppings. They are broken terrain, or one level worse than open. Visibility is for heavy woods, and any unit in them gets a small additional cover bonus for the thick vegetation and rocks.

The cornfields on the map were left standing during the winter. They are light woods for visibility, but do not affect movement rates. The remaining open fields were harvested cornfields and cotton fields.

Deployment

The game begins with the forces set up on the board as shown. McCook and Sheridan are at the Harding House, and Davis is with Carlin. Unfortunately, the Union do not get any reinforcements. The same cannot be said for the Confederates.

Wood's brigade enters immediately on at **1** in line of battle on Turn [1/1/1]. From left to right, they are deployed as: 33rd Alabama, 45th Mississippi, and 16th Alabama. The 9th Texas, from Vaughn's brigade, due to a mix-up, is to the right Wood, and enters with them. As long as they remain in contact with Wood, they can take orders from him. If they become separated normal command and control rules apply. They can return to Vaughn at any time. Vaughn enters next at **2** on Turn [4/3/2]. From left to right they are: 13th, 12th, and 154th Tennessee. Robertson's battery follows in the center.

Next Lucius Polk marches onto the map, as part of the grand flanking movement. His brigade enters at

Major General Benjamin F. Cheatham

3 on Turn [5/4/3]. From left to right the regiments are: 5th Tennessee, 1st Arkansas, 2nd Tennessee, and 13th & 15th Arkansas. Key's battery enters behind them. Maney marches on in line of battle at **4** on Turn [7/5/4] with Smith's battery behind them. The infantry from left to right are: 6th & 9th, 4th, and 1st & 27th Tennessee. Finally, Anderson's brigade enters the battle later in the morning on Turn [19/13/10] at **5** in line of battle. From left to right they are: 43rd Alabama, 29th and 30th Mississippi.

Generals Polk and Cheatham start the game behind Manigault's brigade, giving them an inspiring speech. At Stones River, Withers' Division was deployed in front in a single line, and Cheatham's Division was directly behind it. During the battle, Cheatham was given operational control of the four brigades opposite the Harding House, two of his and two of Withers, while Withers took control of the four brigades north of the Wilkinson Turnpike. As such, Cheatham can benefit all units in Loomis and Manigault's brigades.

Victory Conditions

The objective of the Confederates is to push the Union off the board before the end of the game at 11 o'clock. The Union have to delay them as much as possible. If the Union are still holding out at the end of the game, add up the Victory Points for enemy units forced out of the game. The side with the most points wins.

Order of Battle

Army of the Cumberland (Fourteenth Corps)

Right Wing
MG Alexander M. McCook [+1]

First Division
BG Jefferson C. Davis [+2]

2nd Brigade	ES	20	30	40	50	100	Status	Arm.
Col. William P. Carlin [+1]	1,668	83	56	42	33	17		
21st Illinois	598	30	20	15	12	6	3	R
38th Illinois	302	15	10	8	6	3	3	R
101st Ohio	461	23	15	12	9	5	3	R
15th Wisconsin	307	15	10	8	6	3	3	R
	ES	Status	Armament					
2nd Minnesota Battery		3	**4x** 6 lb. SB, **2x** 12 lb. H					

3rd Brigade	ES	20	30	40	50	100	Status	Arm.
Col. William E. Woodruff [+1]	1,331	67	44	33	27	13		
25th Illinois	439	22	15	11	9	4	3	R
35th Illinois	397	20	13	10	8	4	3	R
81st Indiana	495	25	17	12	10	5	2	R
	ES	Status	Armament					
8th Wisconsin Battery		3	**4x** 3" R, **2x** 12 lb. H					

Third Division
BG Philip H. Sheridan [+3]

1st Brigade	ES	20	30	40	50	100	Status	Arm.
BG Joshua W. Sill [+1]	1,839	86	57	43	34	17		
36th Illinois	375	19	13	9	8	4	4	R
88th Illinois	432	22	14	11	9	4	3	R
21st Michigan	444	22	15	11	9	4	3	R
24th Wisconsin	468	23	16	12	9	5	3	R
	ES	Status	Armament					
4th Indiana Battery	120	3	**2x** 6 lb. SB, **2x** 6 lb. JR					

An example of the cedar breaks and forest in the Murfreesboro area. Thick cedars with small openings on limestone flats. You can see how visibility would be extremely limited in terrain like this.

2nd Brigade Col. Frederick Schaefer [+1]	ES	20	30	40	50	100	Status	Arm.
	1,561	78	52	39	31	16		
44th Illinois	395	20	13	10	8	4	3	R
73rd Illinois	437	22	15	11	9	4	3	R
2nd Missouri	307	15	10	8	6	3	3	R
15th Missouri	422	21	14	11	8	4	3	R
	ES	Status	Armament					
Battery G, 1st Missouri		3	**2x** 10 lb. P, **4x** 12 lb. H					

3rd Brigade Col. George W. Roberts [+1]	ES	20	30	40	50	100	Status	Arm.
	1,520	71	47	35	28	14		
22nd Illinois	342	17	11	9	7	3	3	R
27th Illinois	289	14	10	7	6	3	3	R
42nd Illinois	347	17	12	9	7	3	3	R
51st Illinois	432	22	14	11	9	4	3	R
	ES	Status	Armament					
Battery C, 1st Illinois	110	3	**4x** 3" R, **2x** 12 lb. H					

Army of Tennessee

Polk's Corps
LG Leonidas Polk [+2]

Cheatham's Division
MG Benjamin F. Cheatham [+2]

Third Brigade BG George E. Maney [+1]	ES	20	30	40	50	100	Status	Arm.
	1,382	65	43	33	26	13		
1st & 27th Tennessee	457	23	15	11	9	5	3	R
4th Tennessee (PA), Maney's SS	432	22	14	11	9	4	3	R
6th & 9th Tennessee	412	21	14	10	8	4	3	M

	ES	Status	Armament
Smith's Mississippi Battery	81	3	**2x** 6 lb. SB, **2x** 12 lb. H

Fourth Brigade Col. Alfred J. Vaughn Jr. [+1]	ES	20	30	40	50	100	Status	Arm.
	1,692	85	56	42	34	17		
12th Tennessee	322	16	11	8	6	3	3	R
13th, 29th Tennessee	506	25	17	13	10	5	3	M
154th, 47th Tennessee	541	27	18	14	11	5	3	R
9th Texas	323	16	11	8	6	3	3	R

First Brigade (Withers' Division) Col. John Q. Loomis [+1]	ES	20	30	40	50	100	Status	Arm.
	2,330	110	74	55	44	22		
19th Alabama	530	27	18	13	11	5	3	R
22nd Alabama, 17th Alabama SS	337	17	11	8	7	3	3	M
25th Alabama, 1st Louisiana Regulars	511	26	17	13	10	5	3	R
26th Alabama	405	20	14	10	8	4	3	R
39th Alabama	422	21	14	11	8	4	2	M

	ES	Status	Armament
Robertson's Florida Battery	125	3	**6x** 12 lb. N

Fourth Brigade (Withers' Division)	ES	20	30	40	50	100	Status	Arm.
Col. Arthur M. Manigault [+1]	2,063	98	65	49	39	20		
24th Alabama	447	22	15	11	9	4	2	R
28th Alabama	459	23	15	11	9	5	2	M
34th Alabama	406	20	14	10	8	4	2	R
10th & 19th South Carolina	651	33	22	16	13	7	2	M

	ES	Status	Armament					
Water's Alabama Battery	100	3	2x 6 lb. SB, 4x 12 lb. H					

Withers' Division

Third Brigade	ES	20	30	40	50	100	Status	Arm.
BG J. Patton Anderson [+2]	1,273	64	42	32	25	13		
45th Alabama	448	22	15	11	9	4	3	R
29th Mississippi	396	20	13	10	8	4	2	R
30th Mississippi	429	21	14	11	9	4	3	M

Cleburne's Division

First Brigade	ES	20	30	40	50	100	Status	Arm.
BG Lucius E. Polk [+1]	1,745	83	56	42	33	17		
1st Arkansas	400	20	13	10	8	4	4	R
13th & 15th Arkansas	375	19	13	9	8	4	3	R
5th Tennessee, 5th Confederate	520	26	17	13	10	5	3	R
2nd Tennessee	370	19	12	9	7	4	4	R

	ES	Status	Armament					
Key's Arkansas Battery	80	3	2x 6 lb. SB; 2x 12 lb. H					

Fourth Brigade	ES	20	30	40	50	100	Status	Arm.
BG S. Sterling A. M. Wood [+1]	1,241	62	41	31	25	12		
16th Alabama	406	20	14	10	8	4	3	R
33rd Alabama, 15th AL SS	418	21	14	10	8	4	3	R
45th Mississippi, 3rd Confederate	417	21	14	10	8	4	3	M

Optional Rules

There are no optional rules for this game.

Author's Notes

This is the continuation of the grueling morning attack at Stones River, and the fight where Sheridan won his second star. It's just one sledgehammer blow after another as the rebels pry the Federals from one position to another. It's a good set piece battle for Civil War combat.

Unfortunately, this portion of the battlefield has been entirely paved over with urban development. There are no unit position images available, unless you like looking at pictures of strip malls and brick apartment complexes.

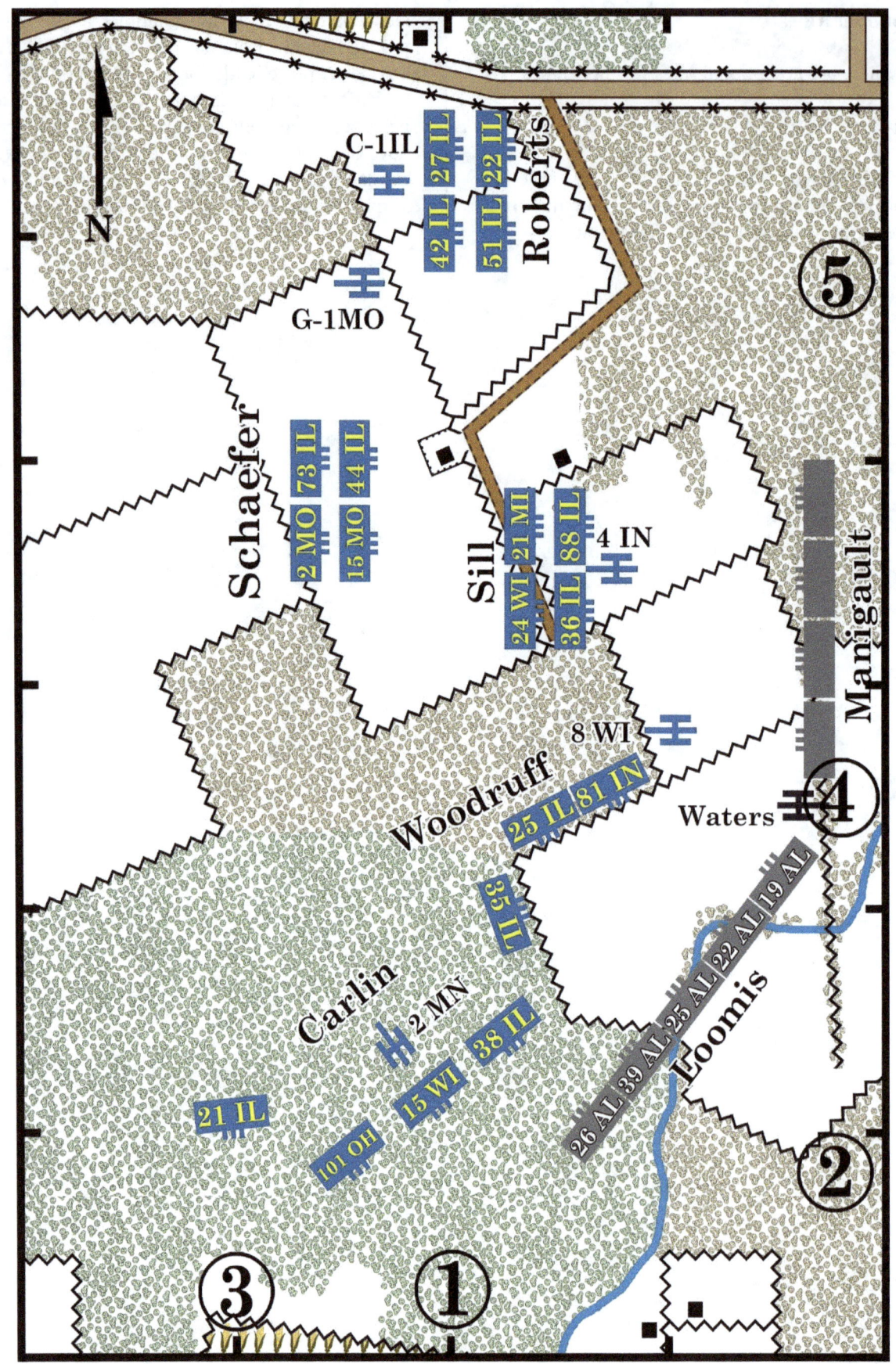

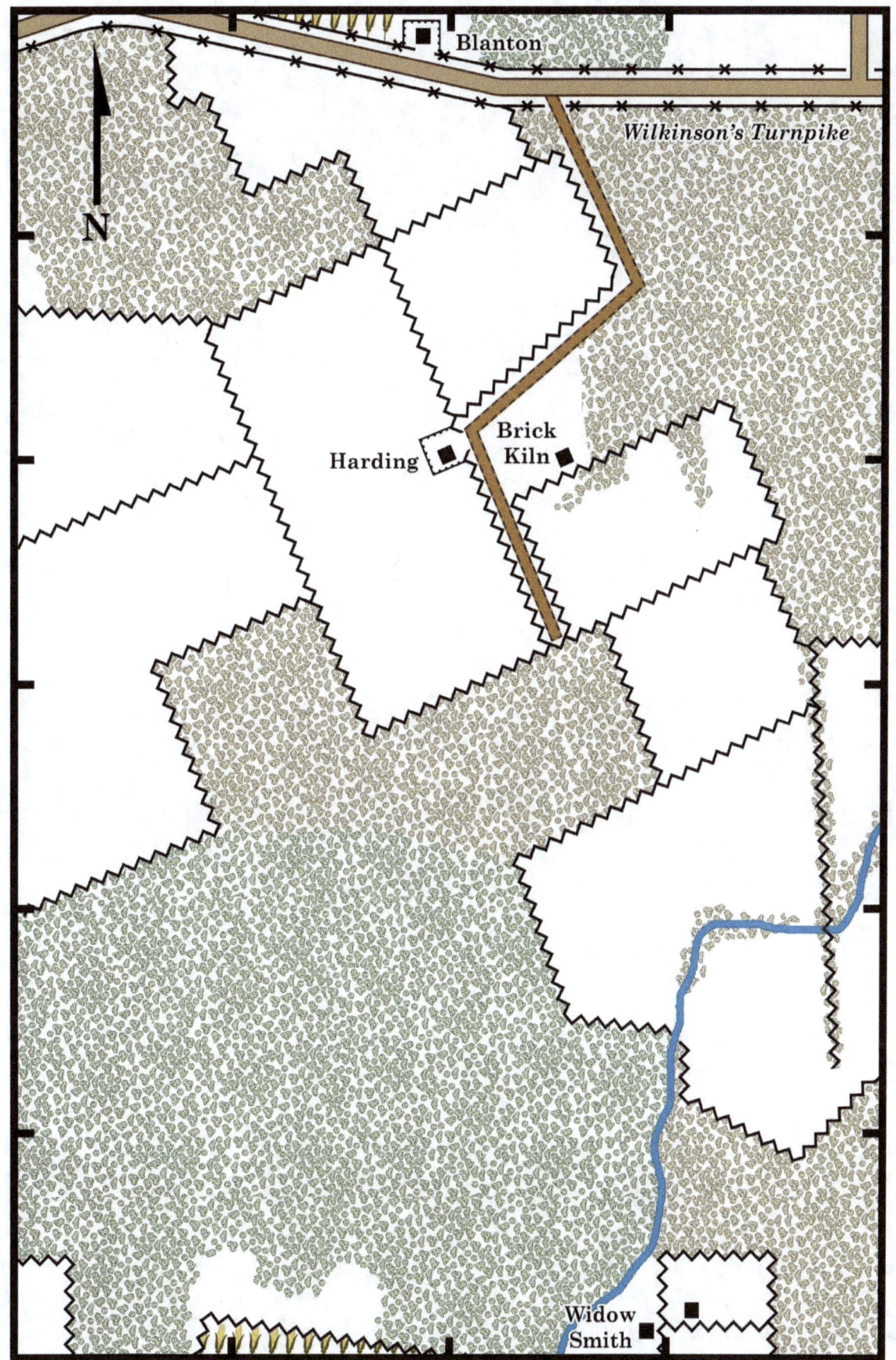

The Battle of Wauhatchie
October 28th, 1863

Background

Following the Union defeat at Chickamauga in late September 1863, General Rosecrans retreated with his Army of the Cumberland into Chattanooga. Chattanooga was a strategic road and rail crossroads on the south side of the Tennessee River. Its possession by the Union would act as a springboard for an invasion of Georgia and the heart of the Confederacy. General Bragg was determined to get it back.

One of the first things Bragg did was cut off Rosecrans' supply lines. The towering heights of Lookout Mountain ended abruptly at the Tennessee River, and since the rebels possessed the mountain, they could interdict any traffic on the river or railroad at its base. They also controlled the south bank of the river, so could fire on traffic on the road on the other side farther upstream. This left Rosecrans with only one link to the outside world for supplies, a winding mountainous road to the north. This was vulnerable to Confederate cavalry, which did strike several times. It was imperative to open a secure line for the beleaguered army.

The Lincoln administration and War Department took decisive action. First, they detached the Eleventh and Twelfth Corps from the Army of the Potomac in Virginia and sent them by rail to northern Alabama on the way to Chattanooga. Second, Major General Ulysses S. Grant, commander of all Union forces west of the Appalachian Mountains, relived Rosecrans from command. In his place he elevated Major General George H. Thomas to command the Army of the Cumberland.

Thomas immediately launched a plan Rosecrans had been preparing. In the predawn hours of October 27th one brigade sailed down the river on pontoon boats, and landed at Brown's Ferry northwest of the town. Another marched to a point opposite them. They overwhelmed the Confederate skirmishers and used the pontoons to construct a bridge.

Brigadier General John W. Geary

At the same time Major General Joseph E. Hooker and the two corps from the Army of the Potomac approached Lookout Valley, on the west side of the mountain, from the southwest. During the day Hooker's force marched northward up the valley, and linked up with the Army of the Cumberland at Brown's Ferry. The "Cracker Line," as it was coined, was open. At least tenuously.

Bragg was determined to break it again. He ordered Lieutenant General James Longstreet to move into the Valley and break the line again. The high command had observed from Lookout Mountain that a small Union detachment had been left at Wauhatchie Station, where the Nashville and Chattanooga Railroad met the Trenton Railroad spur. Brigadier General Micah Jenkin's division moved out after dark to destroy the isolated outpost.

Brigadier General John W. Geary and his division had been left behind to protect the railroad junction, as well as secure the southern reaches of Lookout Valley. Unfortunately, the fighting at Gettysburg, the rapid movement to Georgia, and the need to leave detachments to guard the railroad behind them severely depleted the division's strength. The two brigades in his division barely equaled one mid-sized brigade.

Jenkins entered the valley and sent two brigades to block Hooker at Brown's Ferry, one to destroy Geary, with his fourth in reserve. He sent Col. John Bratton's South Carolina brigade

Looking south down the Wauhatchie Road towards the Union position. The Federals focal point was the high ground across the road. This was the Confederate point of view, although at night.

to attack Geary. Bratton first contacted Geary's skirmishers around 10 p.m., but didn't get the attack fully underway until after midnight. The fighting was confusing and fierce in the dark night. Volleys were aimed at the opposing muzzle flashes. The single battery at Geary's disposal helped keep the Confederate at bay.

Still, Bratton's line gradually began to overlap Geary's, especially once Bratton received reinforcements from a regiment he had left behind to guard his rear. The Union line bent back and took fire from three sides. General Geary's son, commanding an artillery section, was shot down and died in his father's arms. It looked like the rebels might emerge triumphant, but then Bratton received word that the enemy was marching from the north towards his position. Hooker had been fighting much of the night to reach Geary in a series of assaults to open the road. Bratton reluctantly broke off the engagement a little after 3 a.m. Unsuccessful, Jenkins was forced to retreat across Lookout Creek and back to the slopes of Lookout Mountain. The direct road back to Nashville was opened, this time for good.

Game Overview

This game is a brigade vs. brigade action. The board is small, and it should be a quick game. However, it is also fought entirely at night, which may slow things down a bit. It would also be a perfect game to use hidden movement rules.

The game table is 3' x 4'. The game begins at 12:15 a.m. and ends at 3:30 a.m. on Turn [20/14/11].

Terrain

The map is generally flat, with a few hills along the edges and some small rises in the middle. The hills are low and flat, only ¼ inch in height, or ½ at most. They deduct an inch from movement going uphill. The streams are shallow, and cost an inch to cross. The woods are open. They deduct an inch from open terrain movement, and are light woods for visibility (but are superseded by night visibility rules). The railroad and plowed field do not affect the game.

The entire battle is fought at night. If the rules being played do not include night guidelines, consider the following.

Colonel John Bratton

Night
- Visibility is the same as heavy woods.
- Quarter unit firing strengths.
- Halve movement rates.
- Impose a small penalty for attempting to reform from disorder.

Deployment

Set up the game as shown. The Union are in position. Battery E, Pennsylvania Light is limbered and ready to move. The Federals also have a supply wagon. It moves as heavy artillery, and units can resupply form it by spending a full turn next to it. The Confederates can also capture it by killing the drivers just like firing on limbered artillery, and spending a full turn next to it.

The brigade commanders can be with any of their units. Geary and Major Reynolds start next to the battery.

Bratton gets reinforcements when the 6th South Carolina enters at **1** on Turn [10/7/5]. They can be in any formation, even march column on the road as needed.

Victory Conditions

The game continues until the Union are destroyed or forced off the board, or the Confederates take some many casualties they can no longer continue. Bratton must withdraw at the end of Turn [20/14/11]. The Union either survives and wins, or perishes and loses the game. There is no in-between.

Order of Battle

Army of the Potomac

*Hooker's Command**

*Reinforcements from the Army of the Potomac not yet formally integrated into the Army of the Cumberland

Twelfth Corps

Second Division
BG John W. Geary [+2]

2nd Brigade	ES	20	30	40	50	100	Status	Arm.
Col. George A. Cobham, Jr. [+1]	803	40	27	20	16	8		
29th Pennsylvania	387	19	13	10	8	4	3	R
109th, 111th Pennsylvania	416	21	14	10	8	4	3	R

The view from the Union position along the slope of the hill next to the Wauhatchie Road. The Confederates approached along the road in the distance. The Nashville and Chattanooga Railroad is just to the right behind the trees. The postwar New York monument to its veterans is to the left.

3rd Brigade	ES	20	30	40	50	100	Status	Arm.
BG George S. Greene [+1]	785	39	26	20	16	8		
78th, 149th New York	412	21	14	10	8	4	3	R
137th New York	373	19	12	9	7	4	4	R

Maj. John A. Reynolds [+1]	ES	Status	Armament
Battery E, Pennsylvania Light		4	**4x** 12 lb. N

Army of Tennessee

Longstreet's Corps
Hood's Division

Jenkin's Brigade	ES	20	30	40	50	100	Status	Arm.
Col. John Bratton [+1]	1,954	98	65	49	39	20		
1st South Carolina	377	19	13	9	8	4	3	R
2nd South Carolina Rifles	279	14	9	7	6	3	3	R
5th South Carolina	406	20	14	10	8	4	3	R
6th South Carolina	313	16	10	8	6	3	3	R
Hampton's Legion	388	19	13	10	8	4	3	R
Palmetto Sharpshooters	191	10	6	5	4	2	3	R

Optional Rules

There are no real optional rules for this game. However, it would be an excellent opportunity to use hidden movement rules.

Author's Notes

I love small unit actions, and single brigade fights. Not every fight was a contest between armies, corps, or even divisions. Small fights were common, and they are easy to game. Plus, it forces you to think like a brigade commander. The Wauhatchie battle being fought at night makes it even more interesting.

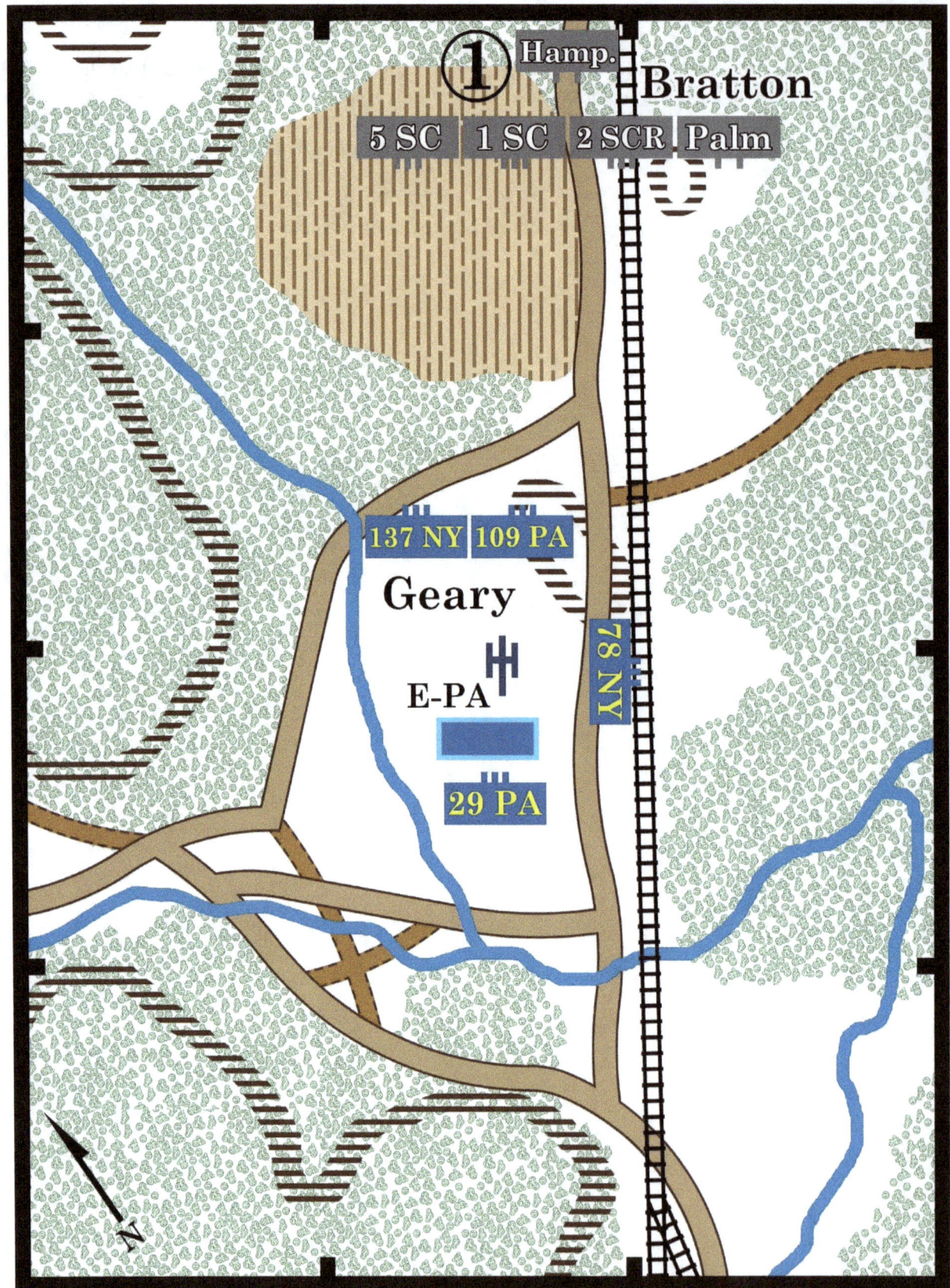

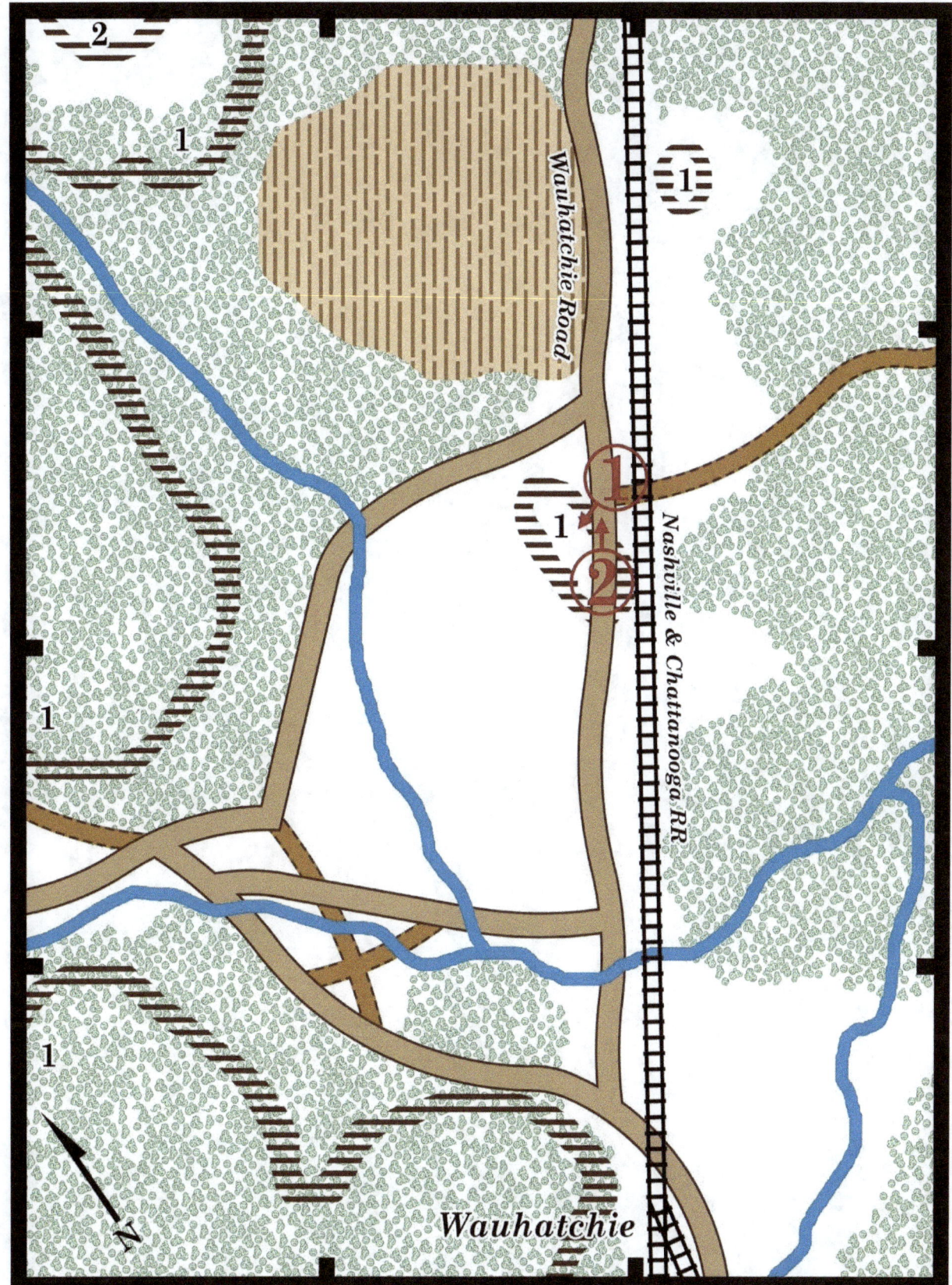

The Battle of Fort Sanders
November 29th, 1863

Background

The liberation of East Tennessee was a war aim for Abraham Lincoln from the start of the war. The area had high Union sentiment, and Lincoln consistently pressured his commanders to invade and free the area. The logistical obstacles were immense, however. Any advance would have to be over the mountains between Kentucky and Tennessee. Then any supplies would have to travel over those same mountains, vulnerable to attack. It was mid-August 1863 before Major General Ambrose E. Burnside felt ready to begin his advance.

On August 16th Burnside's Army of the Ohio left Lexington Kentucky on the way south. He bypassed the strongly held Cumberland Gap and approached Knoxville, the economic and cultural center of the region. Despite the mountains, Burnside moved rapidly, and a cavalry brigade entered Knoxville on September 2nd, and his infantry the next day. Most of the infantry and cavalry from the Confederate Department of East Tennessee had been ordered south to link up with Bragg, and would fight with him during the Battle of Chickamauga. Burnside quickly exploited the vacuum, forcing the surrender of the garrison at Cumberland Gap. He then pushed the remaining Confederates back into Virginia. East Tennessee was secured.

General Bragg outside Chattanooga grew concerned that Burnside would move south and reinforce the Union army trapped inside the city. Even after General Grant arrived and the supply line re-opened for the Union, Bragg insisted on retaking East Tennessee. Against his subordinate's objections, he ordered Lieutenant General James Longstreet to take his corps from the Army of Northern Virginia and recapture the region.

Longstreet left in early November, and after a series of smaller battles approached Knoxville on November 17th. He did not have the forces or equipment for a siege, and planned an assault to capture the city. He delayed while awaiting more reinforcements from Bragg, and by the evening

Brigadier General Edward Ferrero

of November 28th was ready. The attack would commence the next day.

The Confederates successfully prepared by vigorously pushing the Union skirmishers back into their entrenchments during the night. Three small Confederate brigades from Major General Lafayette McLaws' Division assembled in a field of dense felled trees and underbrush northeast of the large Fort Sanders, the northwestern angle of the city's defenses. Opposing him was Brigadier General Edward Ferrero's Federal division, stretched thin in a long arc from the Holston River to Second Creek just west of the city. After a short predawn bombardment, the assaulting column leapt forward. They immediately entered a web of telegraph wire strung between tree stumps, disrupting the formation, slowing them down, and prolonging their exposure the Union artillery and rifle fire.

As the rebels entered the ditch surrounding the fort, then found it was much deeper than expected. In addition, the near vertical walls of the fort were frozen and slippery with ice, making digging handholds to climb nearly impossible. No ladders were provided by the Confederate high command, nor fascines to fill and cross the ditch. The ditch became a death trap, with fire coming from multiple directions. A few soldiers made it to the top of the parapet, planting three battle flags, but they were quickly killed, wounded, or captured.

Longstreet had several brigades ready to support his success, but once it became apparent

Viewpoint of the Confederates as they approached Fort Sanders. The stumps are clearly visible, and the northwest bastion of the fort looms in the background. The sentry on top of the parapet provides a good example of scale. This, and the other period photos, were taken in March 1864.

the assault was unsuccessful, he decided not to reinforce his failure. The survivors of the attack broke and ran, falling back to the Confederate lines. Learning that Grant decisively defeated Bragg at Chattanooga, with the latter retreating to Dalton, Georgia, Longstreet decided to move east back into Virginia. Knoxville had held.

Game Overview

This is a small game packed with action. It's about division sized, but many of the component brigades are small affairs, composed of consolidated regiments (for game mechanics, not historically). It's an assault on fortifications.

The game board is 3' x 4' in size. The game begins at 6:00 a.m. and ends when or if the Union are forced to retreat and the Confederates capture Knoxville.

Terrain

The map is mostly open, as the ground has been cleared for development of the city, and by the Union army to construct fortifications and fields of fire. The elevations are ½ inches tall and cost an inch of movement going uphill. The railroad has an embankment at places. This acts as light or hasty works for any infantry unit along the railroad within the embankment. The railroad tracks themselves do not affect the game. The orchard no longer has leaves in the late autumn, and it does not affect line of sight. However, it does provide a small cover bonus for any unit within, or from any fire that passes through it.

The historic network of trails was quite extensive. Feel free to simplify if desired.

The woods are open woods that only deduct an inch from movement. They are light woods for visibility. The area north of the Kingston Road in front of the works was cut down for open fields of fire. They left many of the trees laying down to form obstacles. Any unit moving through this field must make a tactical roll or morale check, whichever is appropriate for the rules. If the unit fails, it goes into disorder. However, any unit in this field automatically gets a cover bonus for the dips and trees. A unit may reform and remain in the desired formation if it remains stationary, but if it moves, then it must roll again. Skirmishers are not affected.

This field ends at the wire entanglements. The Federals stretched telegraph wire between stumps in a vast arc around Fort Sanders. It should be about 3-4 inches wide. The belt narrows as it moves eastward in front of Anderson's Brigade. Any unit moving through this field automatically goes into disorder. Like the field of downed trees, a unit may reform and remain stationary, but once it moves, it will automatically go into disorder

Major General Lafayette McLaws

again. However, there is no cover bonus for downed trees in this area. Skirmishers may move through this area as well without going into disorder.

Fort Sanders and the other forts are heavy works. For Fort Sanders specifically, any unit that moves through or charges over the walls must automatically stop at the ditch, or edge of the fort. It can then move normally the next turn. Standard rules for heavy works apply for the other forts. The connecting trenches are medium works. The Union interior line is hasty works, as are the Confederate works protecting their artillery.

Deployment

Set up the game as shown on the scenario map. Fort Sanders has some nuisances. First, the 79th New York is deployed inside the fort, but not shown on the map for space considerations. It may fit in between the artillery sections where space allows. Second, the artillery sections may fire down the adjacent walls of the fort. For example, the sections of Battery E, 2nd United States may fire down the northwest and southwest faces of the bastions, respectively. Likewise, the sections of Battery D, 1st Rhode Island can fire along both edges of their bastions. On a micro-tactical level, there are embrasures in the fort that allow them to do this, but are impractical to recreate on a game board.

The Confederates begin the game with a short artillery bombardment. McLaw's Division is released on Turn [2/2/2] and may move normally. Kershaw is elsewhere along the line, and is not with his skirmish line. Anderson's Brigade may not move during the normal game. During the actual battle, they did not attack vigorously, if much at all. Also, Anderson's Brigade is far enough within the railroad embankment that it is protected from fire from Fort Zoellner.

Victory Conditions

The game continues until the Union are forced from the board, or the Confederates can no longer advance. There is plenty of daylight and no set end to the game. If the Union can hold out, they win.

Order of Battle

Army of the Ohio

Ninth Corps
First Division
BG Edward Ferrero [+2]

1st Brigade	ES	20	30	40	50	100	Status	Arm.
Col. David Morrison [+1]	646	32	22	16	13	6		
36th Massachusetts, 8th Michigan	344	17	11	9	7	3	3	R
79th New York, 45th Pennsylvania	302	15	10	8	6	3	3	R

Looking east down the face of the northwest bastion of Fort Sanders. This view gives a good look at the ditch and the walls of the fort. The vertical walls of the fort had degraded somewhat between the battle and March 1864 when this photo was taken. The sentry from the previous photo is still standing on the parapet.

2nd Brigade	ES	20	30	40	50	100	Status	Arm.
Col. Benjamin C. Christ [+1]	797	40	27	20	16	8		
29th Massachusetts, 27th Michigan	381	19	13	10	8	4	3	R
46th New York, 50th Pennsylvania	416	21	14	10	8	4	3	R

3rd Brigade	ES	20	30	40	50	100	Status	Arm.
Col. William Humphrey [+0]	881	44	29	22	18	9		
2nd, 17th Michigan	462	23	15	12	9	5	3	R
20th Michigan, 100th Pennsylvania	419	21	14	10	8	4	3	R

Artillery	ES	Status	Armament
Battery L, 2nd New York		3	**4x** 3" R
Battery D, 1st Rhode Island		3	**6x** 12 lb. N

Second Division

Artillery	ES	Status	Armament
Battery E, 2nd United States		3	**4x** 20 lb. P
Batteries L & M, 3rd United States		3	**2x** 10 lb. P

Looking from the walls of Fort Sanders northwest along the northwest bastion. This provides an excellent view of the Confederate approach. The rebels crossed this open field as they charged towards the point of the bastion in the upper right.

Army of Tennessee

Longstreet's Corps

McLaws' Division
MG Lafayette McLaws [+2]

Kershaw's Brigade	ES	20	30	40	50	100	Status	Arm.
	589	29	20	15	12	6		
3rd South Carolina	312	16	10	8	6	3	3	R
7th South Carolina	277	14	9	7	6	3	3	R

Wofford's Brigade	ES	20	30	40	50	100	Status	Arm.
Col. Solon Z. Ruff [+0]	1,212	61	40	30	24	12		
16th Georgia, Cobb's Legion	462	23	15	12	9	5	3	R
18th Georgia, Phillip's Legion	416	21	14	10	8	4	3	M
24th Georgia, 3rd GA Bn. SS	334	17	11	8	7	3	3	R

Humphreys' Brigade	ES	20	30	40	50	100	Status	Arm.
BG Benjamin G. Humphreys [+1]	898	45	30	22	18	9		
13th, 17th Mississippi	435	22	15	11	9	4	3	R
18th, 21st Mississippi	463	23	15	12	9	5	3	R

Bryan's Brigade	ES	20	30	40	50	100	Status	Arm.
BG Goode Bryan [+1]	731	37	24	18	15	7		
50th, 51st Georgia	445	22	15	11	9	4	3	R
53rd Georgia	286	14	10	7	6	3	3	R

Hood's Division

Anderson's Brigade	ES	20	30	40	50	100	Status	Arm.
BG George T. Anderson [+1]	1,504	75	50	38	30	15		
7th Georgia	321	16	11	8	6	3	3	R
8th Georgia	385	19	13	10	8	4	3	R
9th Georgia	378	19	13	9	8	4	3	R
11th, 59th Georgia	420	21	14	11	8	4	3	R

Artillery	ES	Status	Armament
Col. Edward P. Alexander [+1]			
Taylor's Virginia Battery		3	**4x** 12 lb. N
Woolfolk's Virginia Battery		3	**4x** 20 lb. P

Optional Rules

There are several optional variations for this game. All must be agreed upon by both sides before the start of the game.

First, Anderson's Brigade may be released. They can begin moving forward on Turn [5/4/3].

If Anderson's Brigade is released, it should be coupled with Union reinforcements arriving from farther down the Union line. Siegfried's Second Division brigade enters at on the trail at **1** on Turn [7/5/4].

Ninth Corps

Second Division

1st Brigade	ES	20	30	40	50	100	Status	Arm.
Col. Joshua K. Sigfried [+1]	727	36	24	18	15	7		
21st Massachusetts, 2nd Maryland	352	18	12	9	7	4	3	R
48th Pennsylvania	375	19	13	9	8	4	3	R

Finally, to really pile on the Union, Longstreet can commit Bushrod Johnson's division to the fight. This can be done with or without releasing Anderson's Brigade. If Johnson's men arrive, they enter at **2** on Turn [8/6/5]. They can be in any formation. It will be a very tough game for the Union if all of the Confederate forces are made available.

Buckner's Division

BG Bushrod R. Johnson [+2]

Johnson's Brigade	ES	20	30	40	50	100	Status	Arm.
Col. John Fulton [+1]	1,084	54	36	27	22	11		
17th & 23rd Tennessee	333	17	11	8	7	3	4	R
25th & 44th Tennessee	354	18	12	9	7	4	3	R
63rd Tennessee	397	20	13	10	8	4	3	R

Gracie's Brigade	ES	20	30	40	50	100	Status	Arm.
BG Archibald Gracie Jr. [+1]	0	77	51	39	31	15		
41st Alabama	385	19	13	10	8	4	3	R
43rd Alabama	416	21	14	10	8	4	3	R
1st & 2nd Bns. Hilliard Legion	368	18	12	9	7	4	3	R
3rd & 4th Bns. Hilliard Legion	372	19	12	9	7	4	3	R

Author's Notes

With Fort Sanders, the Confederates have to assault earthworks for a change. Sanders was a relatively large fortification, and heavily defended by artillery. The infantry on both sides were worn out from months of active campaigning, and individual regiments were small, hence the consolidations for the game to make decent size, playable units. Still, it's going to be a tough battle for the Confederates playing the historical scenario without the optional reinforcements.

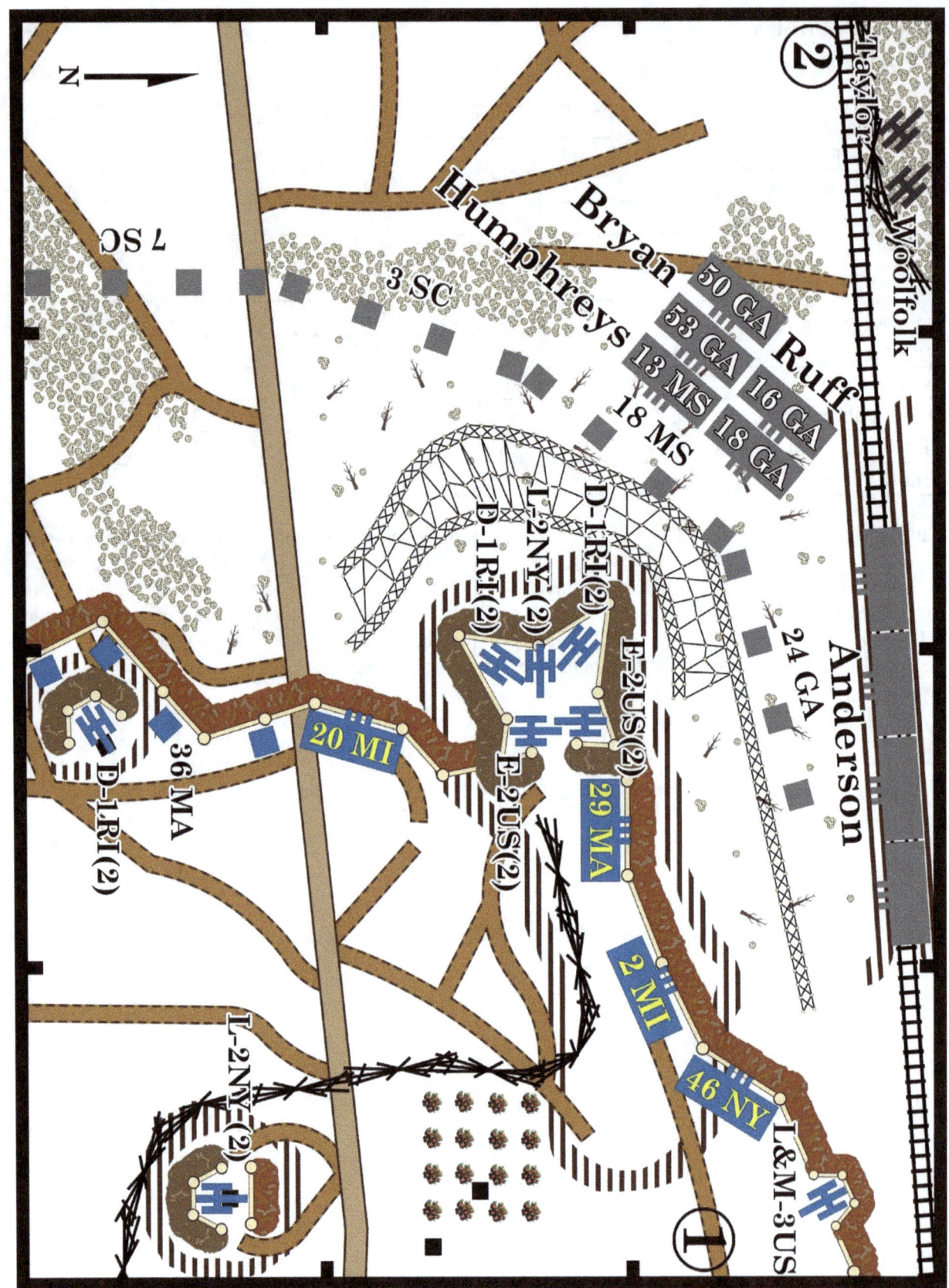

The Third Battle of Murfreesboro
December 7th, 1864

Background

The fall of Atlanta in September 1864 led to a turning point in the respective commander's strategic outlook and decisions. Major General William T. Sherman chose to build up supplies and march to the Atlantic Ocean, cutting a swath through Georgia. General John B. Hood, now commanding the Army of Tennessee, chose to first cut off Sherman's supply line in North Georgia, which Sherman chased off, then moved into northern Alabama. From there he decided to ignore Sherman and invade Tennessee, fancifully hoping it would bring the state back into Confederate control and disrupt Sherman.

Hood outmaneuvered Union commanders until they made a stand at Franklin, Tennessee on November 30th. There Hood assaulted an isolated Union army behind entrenchments with its back to a river. The results devastated the Army of Tennessee. Casualties were severe, and the officer corps was shattered. The Union army escaped that night and retired to Nashville. Hood pursued, hoping to invest the city.

The railroad network and Union outposts concerned Hood. On December 2nd he ordered Major General William B. Bate to march his division to Murfreesboro, then return to Nashville burning bridges and destroying the railroad on the way. On December 4th Bate attacked the blockhouse guarding the railroad bridge at Overall Creek, six miles from Nashville. The Union garrison held the Confederate attacks. On December 5th Bate successfully attacked several blockhouses and bridges in outlying areas to the northwest. Major General Nathan B. Forrest arrived with two divisions of cavalry and two more infantry brigades. However, by this stage of the war these brigades, including Bate's division as well, were shadows of their former selves. Most were no larger than an infantry regiment. Forrest took command of the overall expedition by seniority of rank. He decided, against Bate's judgment, to stop destroying the railroad and

Major General Robert H. Milroy

attack Murfreesboro directly, hoping to capture the large garrison.

By the evening of the 5th Forrest had driven the Union outposts back into Murfreesboro and the large Fortress Rosecrans. The next day was spent with desultory skirmishing. However, Major General Lovell H. Rousseau, the commander at Murfreesboro, refused to surrender the initiative. On the morning of the 7th, he ordered Major General Robert H. Milroy to take two brigades and "make a reconnaissance and feel the enemy in the vicinity." Milroy left Murfreesboro on the Salem Turnpike to the southwest. At the Spence residence he learned there was cavalry farther out, and that the main Confederate body was to the north along the Wilkinson Turnpike. He resumed his march north cross country, but not before detailing a company to drive "sixty fine, fat hogs, belonging to Mr. Spence, that would have fallen into the hands of the enemy if left."

Milroy approached Bate's position as he neared the Giles Harding residence along the Wilkinson Pike. These fields had seen heavy fighting during the December 31st battle. The rebels were behind hastily constructed log barricade facing the open fields. Milroy deployed and shelled the rebel line with his lone battery, but the artillery soon ran low on ammunition. He decided to withdraw (sending the battery back to Fortress Rosecrans to rearm) out of sight to the east, circle around to the Wilkinson Pike and then redeploy facing due west. This caught Bate off

Looking across the field south of the Wilkinson Turnpike from the Union perspective.

guard and he scrambled to shift north to meet him. Unfortunately, two brigades erroneously shifted too far north, taking themselves out of the immediate vicinity.

Milroy's division left the woods north of the Harding house and moved upon Bate's position. A firefight erupted between the two lines. Just as it appeared the largely green garrison troops would waver, Milroy gave an inspiring speech and the line leapt forward. The grey line buckled and broke just as the two errant brigades returned. Neither Bate nor Forrest could stem the tide and exhort the men to stay. Bate fell back, but Milroy did not pursue.

Forrest then moved his forces northwest towards Nashville. They attempted to resume damaging the railroad, but the weather took a turn for the worse and prevented them from doing so. Hood ordered Bate's Division to return to Nashville on the 9th. The Confederates had destroyed some blockhouse and damaged the railroad, but the garrison and large supply depot at Murfreesboro was saved.

Game Overview

The fight at Third Murfreesboro is a small division-sized affair between largely untested Union garrison troops, and Bate's worn out division. The map size is small and easily manageable. It can be easily played in one session.

The map is 4' x 3'. The game begins at 1:30 p.m. and ends as the sun begins to set on Turn [20/14/11].

Terrain

The board is flat, with the area cut with open fields and wood lots. The brown winter woods deduct an inch from open movement and are light woods for visibility. The green cedar woods are broken, or one terrain value below open. They are heavy woods for visibility, and afford an additional cover bonus because of the dense cedars and limestone outcroppings.

The fences cost an inch of movement to cross. The war has been unkind to the fences in the area. There should be many missing section and random gaps. The Confederate barricades are hasty works.

Deployment

Begin the game with the two forces set up on the map as shown. General Milroy begins on the road between the 8th Minnesota and 181st Ohio. Anderson's brigade enters immediately behind Thomas on Turn [1/1/1]. From left to right they are deployed: 178th Ohio, 12th Indiana Cavalry, and 177th Ohio (north of the turnpike behind the 8th Minnesota). The 12th Indiana Cavalry is dismounted and remains so for the duration of the game.

Major General William B. Bate

The Confederates begin behind their new hasty works. Both Generals Bate and Forrest are with them. Jackson and Sears' brigades return at **1** on Turn [5/4/3], in that order. Finally, Forrest's cavalry belatedly arrives to either stop Milroy from pursuing, or drive him back into Murfreesboro. They enter along the turnpike at **2** on Turn [17/12/9].

Victory Conditions

The game continues until dusk on Turn [20/14/11]. Add up the Victory Points for enemy units removed from the game. The side with the most Victory Points wins.

Order of Battle

Department of the Cumberland, District of Tennessee

Milroy's Division*
MG Robert H. Milroy [+2]

First Brigade	ES	20	30	40	50	100	Status	Arm.
Col. Minor T. Thomas [+0]	1,876	94	63	47	38	19		
8th Minnesota	549	27	18	14	11	5	3	R
61th Illinois	187	9	6	5	4	2	3	R
174th Ohio	575	29	19	14	12	6	2	R
181st Ohio	565	28	19	14	11	6	2	R

Second Brigade	ES	20	30	40	50	100	Status	Arm.
Col. Edward Anderson [+0]	1,326	66	44	33	27	13		
177th Ohio	507	25	17	13	10	5	2	R
178th Ohio	490	25	16	12	10	5	2	R
12th Indiana Cavalry	329	16	11	8	7	3	3	R

*This command was only temporarily created for this specific mission on December 7th.

The open field south of the Wilkinson Turnpike from the Confederate lines. This was one of the few open areas left on this part of the field, but sadly has been developed since this photo was taken.

Army of Tennessee

MG Nathan B. Forrest [+2]*
*In overall command of all Confederate forces

Cheatham's Corps

Bate's Division
MG William B. Bate [+1]

Smith's Brigade	ES	20	30	40	50	100	Status	Arm.
BG Thomas B. Smith [+1]	482	24	16	12	10	5		
Smith	482	24	16	12	10	5	3	R

Finley's Brigade	ES	20	30	40	50	100	Status	Arm.
Col. Jacob A. Lash [+0]	410	21	14	10	8	4		
Finley	410	21	14	10	8	4	2	R

Jackson's Brigade	ES	20	30	40	50	100	Status	Arm.
BG Henry R. Jackson [+1]	657	33	22	16	13	7		
1st & 66th Georgia, 1st Georgia SS	310	16	10	8	6	3	3	R
25th, 29th & 30th Georgia	347	17	12	9	7	3	2	R

Brown's and Reynold's Brigades*	ES	20	30	40	50	100	Status	Arm.
Col. Joseph B. Palmer [+0]	391	20	13	10	8	4		
Palmer	391	20	13	10	8	4	2	R

*Attached from Lee's Corps, Stevenson's division. Commanded by General Bate.

Sears' Brigades*	ES	20	30	40	50	100	Status	Arm.
BG Claudius W. Sears [+1]	810	41	27	20	16	8		
4th, 35th, 36th Mississippi	426	21	14	11	9	4	2	R
39th, 46th Mississippi, 7th MS Bn.	384	19	13	10	8	4	2	R

*Attached from Stewart Corps, French's division. Commanded by General Bate.

Artillery	ES	Status	Armament
Slocumb's Louisiana Battery		3	**3x** 12 lb. N

Cavalry Corps
MG Nathan B. Forrest [+2]*
*Commands both the Cavalry Corps and Bate's Division.

Jackson's Division
BG William H. Jackson [+2]

Finley's Brigade	ES	20	30	40	50	100	Status	Arm.
BG Frank C. Armstrong [+1]	953	48	32	24	19	10		
1st, 2nd Mississippi Cavalry	462	23	15	12	9	5	3	R
28th, Ballentine's Mississippi Cavalry	491	25	16	12	10	5	3	R

Ross' Brigade	ES	20	30	40	50	100	Status	Arm.
BG Lawrence S. Ross [+1]	914	46	30	23	18	9		
3rd, 6th Texas Cavalry	403	20	13	10	8	4	3	R
9th, 27th Texas Cavalry	511	26	17	13	10	5	3	R

Optional Rules

There are no optional rules for this game.

Author's Notes

There is not much written on this little-known battle fought during Hood's Tennessee campaign. It was also fought on the old Stone's River battlefield from two years previous. It's a fun game, in that while the Union garrison force is mostly green garrison troops, the Confederates are equally worn down and war weary. Particularly Bate's Division, as Bate was not well liked.

I also wish to thank the Jasper County Public Library in Indiana for providing me with a map from the Robert H. Milroy collection showing the general's exact route and the location of the battle in relation to the Harding House, Wilkinson Turnpike, and other landmarks of the 1862 battle.

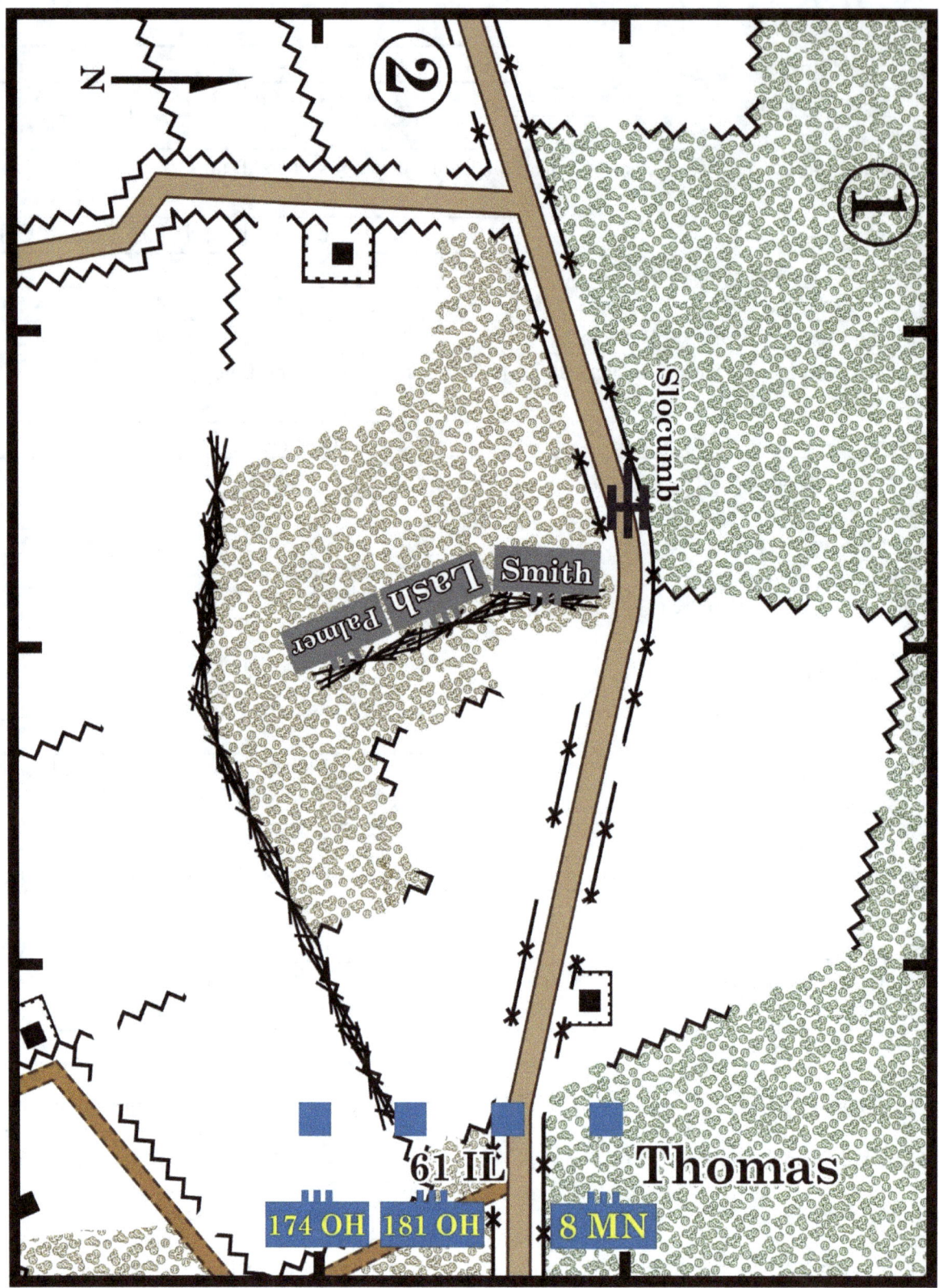

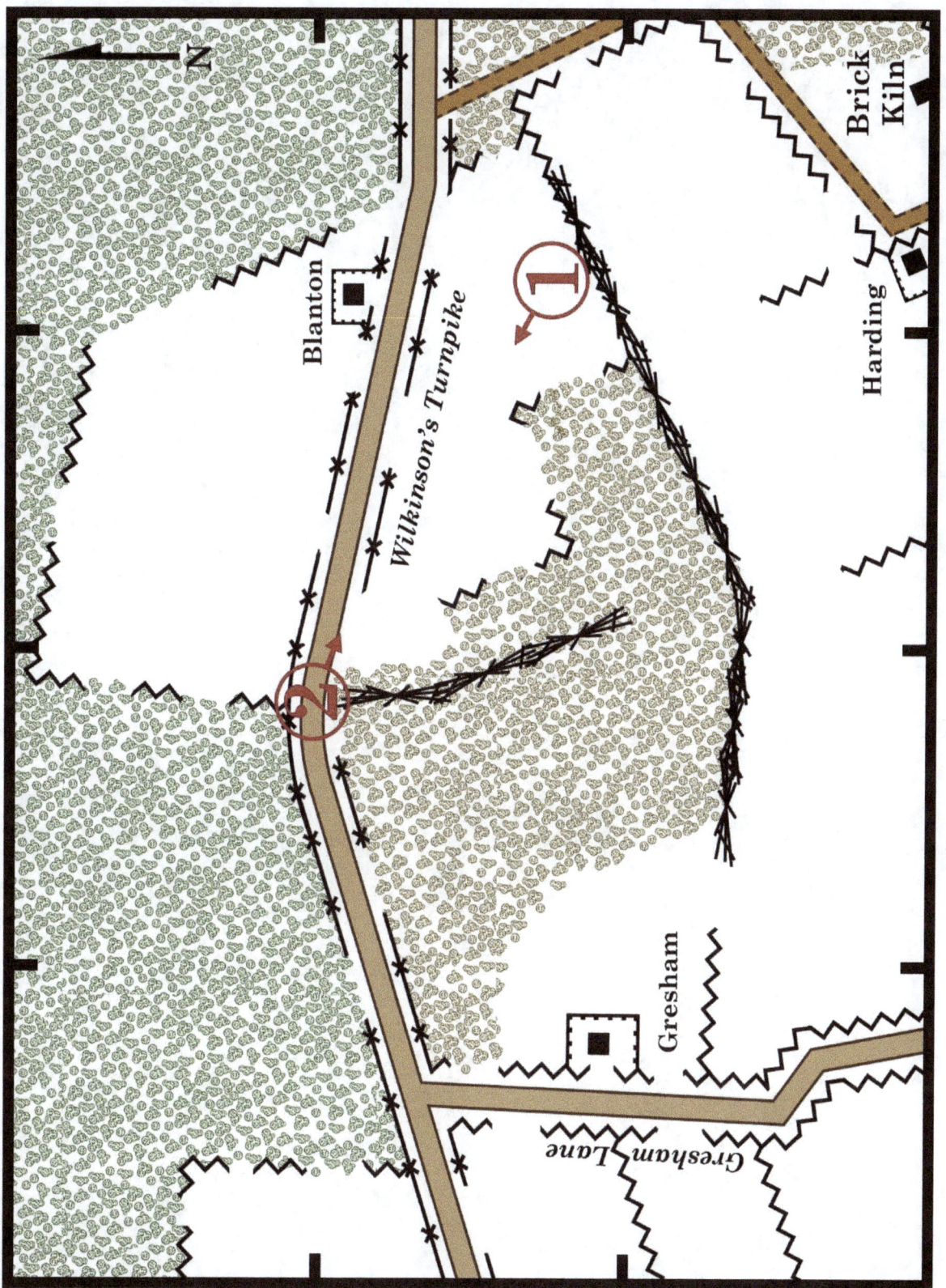

The Battle of Griswoldville
November 22nd, 1864

Background

When General Hood moved into northern Alabama, and then Tennessee after the fall of Atlanta, General Sherman was free to pursue his March to the Sea through Georgia. Sherman's two armies took separate but parallel paths. The Right Wing was the Army of the Tennessee under Major General Oliver O. Howard. They left Atlanta on November, marching south through Lovejoy Station, Jonesboro, and then moving southeast past Macon. Without Hood, Confederate resistance to Sherman's entire force was meager. The only troops at Confederate disposal were several thousand militia, and cavalry.

On November 20th and 21st Union cavalry destroyed Griswoldville, a small settlement east of Macon. Samuel Griswold had built his fortune here, operating a cotton gin factory, grist mills, a general store, post office, and finally, a pistol factory for the Confederacy. In two days, Samuel's legacy was gone. Confederate cavalry arrived to drive the Union away.

Confederate cavalry attacked the 9th Pennsylvania Cavalry along the Gordon Road east of the town on the morning of the 22nd. The grey cavalry forced them back, but the 9th received the aid of the Union 5th Kentucky Cavalry, who in turn forced them to retreat. At this moment Brigadier General Charles C. Wallcutt arrived brigade to help the Union cavalry. His orders were to make a demonstration west towards Macon, to ascertain the strength of the enemy in that area. They drove the Confederates back through Griswoldville. There Wallcutt's division commander ordered him to fall back. Wallcutt retired to a low ridge at the Duncan farm, with a wooded lot behind him, and large open fields to his front. His veterans dug in along the wood line.

In response to the Union thrust, Brigadier General Pleasant J. Philips moved his 1st Division of the Georgia Militia east, through Griswoldville. He intended to deploy and wait for orders, but heard firing ahead. Riding forward, he

Brigadier General Charles C. Wallcutt

found Major Ferdinand W. C. Cook's Athens and Augusta battalions already engaged with Wallcutt's skirmishers. Philips made the decision to deploy and attack the Federals.

Philips got his men into position and advanced. His militia were primary old men and boys, plus factory workers and laborers that so far had escaped Confederate service because of their needed industrial skills. But today they were soldiers, advancing with loaded rifles towards veteran troops behind scratch barricades.

The militia took casualties crossing the open fields, but then advanced into a hollow along a stream bed. There the eastern edge of the ravine shielded them from direct fire. Reforming, Philips charged out of the ravine towards Wallcutt. His veterans delivered a cool, but devasting fire that stopped them in their tracks. They fell back to the ravine, leaving their dead and wounded behind. Walcutt was wounded early in the fight. Still, Philips would not give up. He reformed and made repeated attacks on the Federal lines, with some sources saying up to seven.

During this time, Wallcutt received even more reinforcements. It was just too much for untrained militia, no matter how motivated and courageous they were to defend their homes. As night fell Philips withdrew to the west, back to Macon, leaving a scene of death and destruction. Nothing was gained from Philip's attack, as Macon was never an objective, and Wallcutt was already on his way back to rejoin the main body.

Looking from Wallcutt's line down the road towards the approaching Confederates. The edge of the ravine is at the wood line.

Looking out at the carnage, Lieutenant Charles W. Willis of the 103rd Illinois wrote, "Old grey haired and weakly looking men and young boys not over 15 years old, lay dead or writhing in pain. I hope we will never have to shoot at such men again."

Game Overview

This is a small brigade-sized battle, pitting Confederate militia against veteran Union troops. It's a test that even the best wargamers will find challenging to win as the Confederates.

The map is 3" x 4". The game begins at 2:30 p.m. and ends as the sun begins to set at 5:30 p.m. on Turn [19/13/10].

Terrain

The map is simple, with a single creek and the ridge above it upon which the Union are deployed. The elevations are gentle, ½ inches. Marching uphill costs and inch of movement. The creek deducts and inch from movement as well. The woods are open winter woods, again only costing an inch from open terrain movement. Visibility is for light woods. The swamp is rough terrain.

The area to the east of the creek and the edge of the ravine is a dead zone. Units in that zone are out of the line of sight and shielded from infantry fire, but not artillery. Its assumed timed fuses can still inflict casualties. However, it would still be area or blind fire, whatever the rules call for.

Wallcutt's brigade is behind hasty works. The railroad bridge is destroyed and cannot be used.

Deployment

Begin the game as set up on the scenario map. Wallcutt received reinforcements throughout the late afternoon. The 12th Indiana arrives on the road at **1** on Turn [8/6/5]. Murray's cavalry arrives at **1** on Turn [14/10/8].

Victory Conditions

The game ends if the Union are forced from the board, or the Confederates can no longer continue. If neither occurs, the game ends at 5:30 p.m. on Turn [19/13/10]. If the game ends because of time, add together the Victory Points for enemy units removed from the game. The side with the most Victory Points wins.

Order of Battle

Army of the Tennessee

Fifteenth Army Corps
First Division

1st Brigade	ES	20	30	40	50	100	Status	Arm.
12th Indiana	312	16	10	8	6	3	3	R

2nd Brigade	ES	20	30	40	50	100	Status	Arm.
BG Charles C. Walcutt [+1]	1,663	83	55	42	33	17		
40th Illinois, 46th Ohio*	474	24	16	12	9	5	3	R
103rd Illinois, 6th Iowa	446	22	15	11	9	4	3	R
97th Indiana	391	20	13	10	8	4	3	R
100th Indiana	352	18	12	9	7	4	3	R

*The 46th Ohio was armed with 186 Spencer Repeating Rifles. Provide the combined regiments with a firing bonus.

Cavalry Corps
Third Division

1st Brigade	ES	20	30	40	50	100	Status	Arm.
Col. Eli H. Murray [+1]	733	37	24	18	15	7		
5th Kentucky Cavalry	351	18	12	9	7	4	3	BC
9th Pennsylvania Cavalry	382	19	13	10	8	4	3	BC

Artillery	ES	Status	Armament
Battery B, 1st Michigan		3	2x 3" R

Georgia Militia

1st Division	ES	20	30	40	50	100	Status	Arm.
BG Pleasant J. Philips [+0]	2,352	118	78	59	47	24		
Second Brigade	460	23	15	12	9	5	1	R
Third Brigade	529	26	18	13	11	5	1	R
Fourth Brigade	479	24	16	12	10	5	1	R
Georgia State Line	499	25	17	12	10	5	2	R
Cook's Battalions	385	19	13	10	8	4	1	R

The view from the Confederate line towards the Duncan farm and the Union line. Wallcutt's men were behind crude breastworks at the far wood line.

Artillery	ES	Status	Armament
Anderson's Georgia Battery		3	**4x** 12 lb. N

Optional Rules

There are no optional rules for this game.

Author's Notes

Griswoldville is a fascinating look at veterans vs. militia. It's almost impossible for the Confederates to win. I hesitated to even include this scenario in the book, but it is just so well documented, and unique, and the battlefield is well preserved, that I decided to include it.

The regimental strengths are well documented, but are all in enlisted men. The only reason the values are in red is because of the best guess at adding officers. Otherwise, they are reasonably accurate.

Because of the impossibility of a Confederate victory, this book has an enchantment upon it.* Win as the Confederates, and forever be known for your wargaming prowess.

"Whosoever wins Griswoldville as the Confederates, if they be worthy and played fair, shall earn the title of First Among Wargamers"

---

*For those with strict religious faiths, no not really. There is no "enchantment" on this book. It's just a funny joke and a play on words of a certain fictional god's hammer.

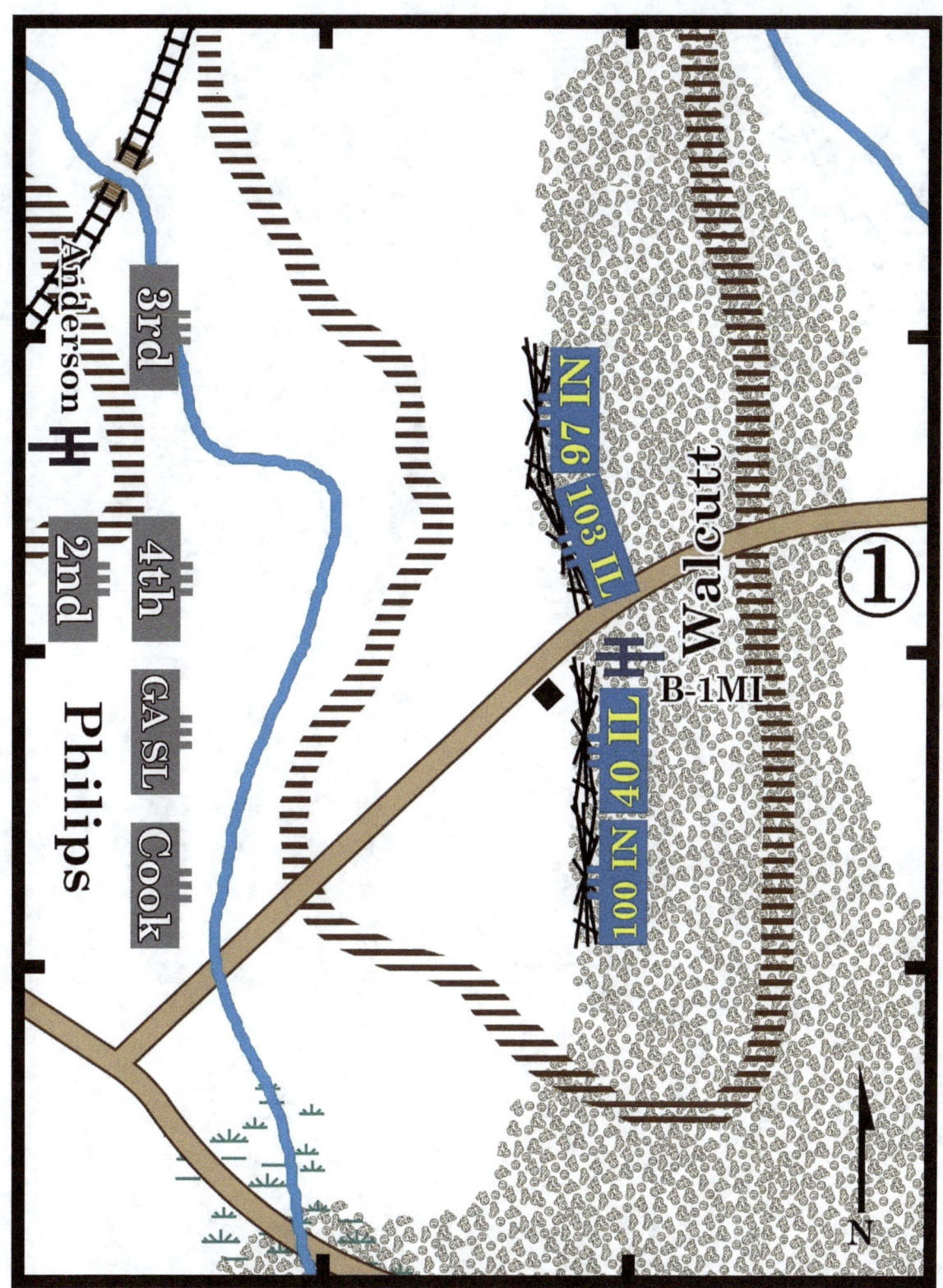

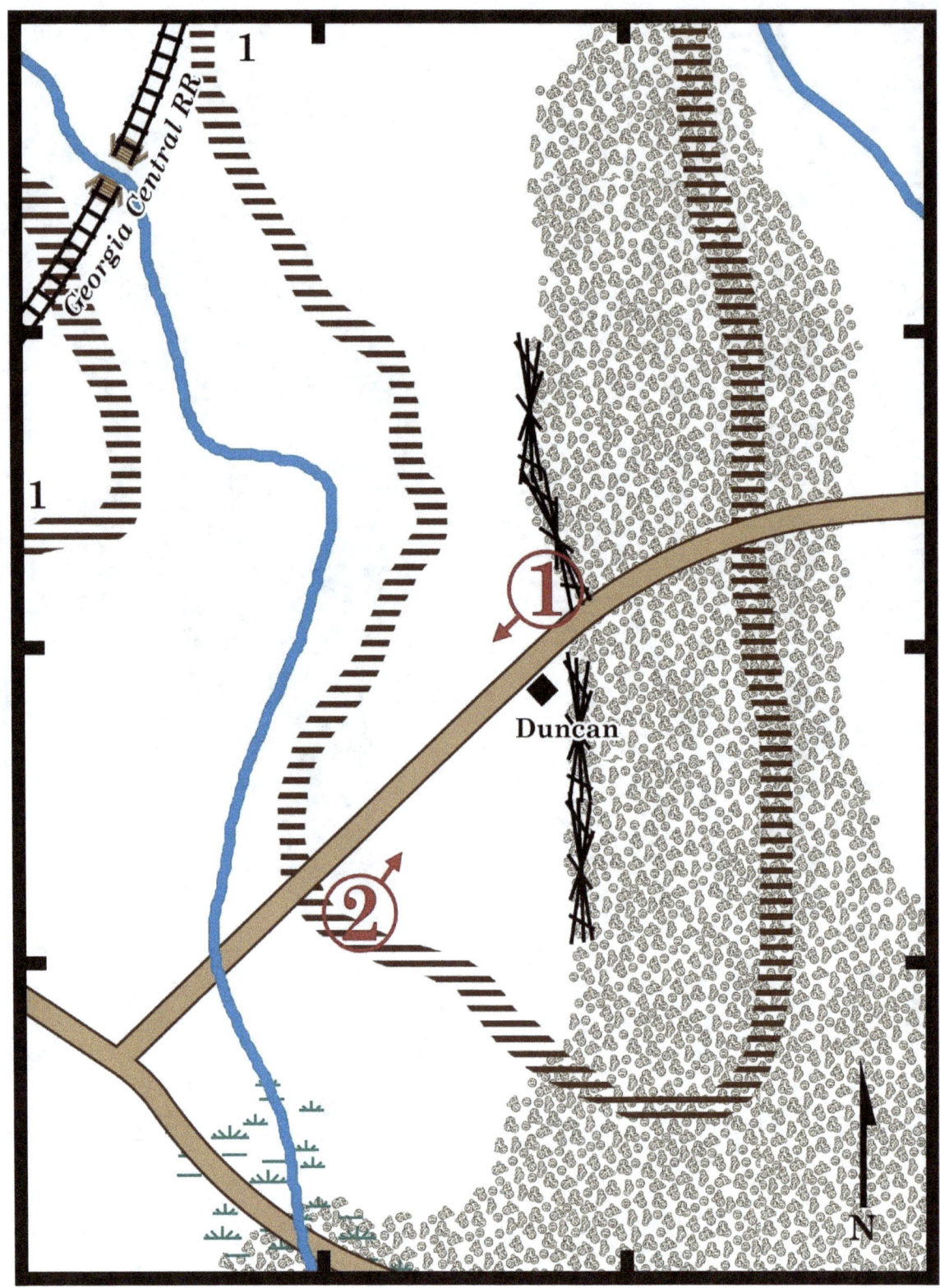

Ride to the Death:
Regimental Wargame Cavalry Scenarios For the American Civil War

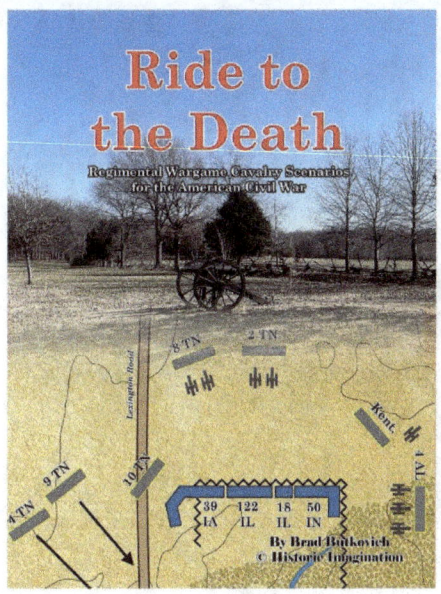

Stock # HI0018

ISBN 13: 978-1-7325976-4-8

The use of cavalry during the American Civil War is often overlooked and one of the least understood and aspects of the war. They were critical in scouting the enemy, finding a flank, and raiding deep into hostile territory to destroy infrastructure or capture supplies.

This scenario book contains rules to play sixteen cavalry battles during the American Civil War, including previously published and brand new scenarios. They have been updated with new information and the maps have been reworked to current standards. If you want to fight a Civil War cavalry battle, this book is for you!

These miniature wargame scenarios are designed to be used with almost any American Civil War regimental or brigade level set of rules. Rules are included for figures based on 20, 30, 40, 50, and 100 historic men per figure/stand. Times are given for 10, 15, and 20 minutes per game turn. Maps are in full color, as are the numerous color photographs of the modern battlefields.

This book does not contain rules for playing miniature wargames.

Available at Amazon.com, other online retailers, as well as your local gaming store (with the ISBN number above).

Also available for download at www.wargamevault.com

Forlorn Hope:
Regimental Wargame Scenarios for the Mississippi River Campaigns: 1861-1863

Stock # HI0020

ISBN 13: 979-8-9904149-1-4

The campaigns and battles along the Mississippi River during the American Civil War were arguably the most important and decisive of the conflict. Even more so than the struggles in the east between the two nation's capitals. It took two years for the Union to finally free the Mississippi from Confederate's domination and blockade. However, once free to Union traffic, it irrevocably split the Confederacy in two, a major blow to both military and commercial operations.

This scenario book contains rules to play fifteen battles along the Mississippi River in the years long struggle to open the vital waterway for the Union. They range from assaulting heavy siege lines, to the bayou low country, to urban combat.

These miniature wargame scenarios are designed to be used with almost any American Civil War regimental or brigade level set of rules. Rules are included for figures based on 20, 30, 40, 50, and 100 historic men per figure/stand. Times are given for 10, 15, and 20 minutes per game turn. Maps are in full color, as are the numerous color photographs of the modern battlefields.

Available at Amazon.com, other online retailers, as well as your local gaming store (with the ISBN number above).

Also available for download at www.wargamevault.com

www.ingramcontent.com/pod-product-compliance
Lightning Source LLC
LaVergne TN
LVHW061938070526
838199LV00060B/3863